ANDREW ZIMMERN'S
bizarre world of food
BRAINS, BUGS, & BLOOD SAUSAGE

ANDREW ZiMMERN'S
bizarre world of food
BRAINS, BUGS, & BLOOD SAUSAGE

ANDREW ZIMMERN

EMBER

Text copyright © 2011 by Andrew Zimmern
Cover photograph copyright © 2011 by The Travel Channel, L.L.C.

All rights reserved. Published in the United States by Ember, an imprint of
Random House Children's Books, a division of Random House, Inc., New York.
Originally published in hardcover in the United States by Delacorte Press,
an imprint of Random House Children's Books, New York, in 2011.

Ember and the colophon are trademarks of Random House, Inc.

Insert photographs courtesy of The Travel Channel, L.L.C.

Visit us on the Web! randomhouse.com/kids and randomhouse.com/teens

Educators and librarians, for a variety of teaching tools,
visit us at randomhouse.com/teachers

The Library of Congress has cataloged the hardcover
edition of this work as follows:
Zimmern, Andrew.
[Bizarre world of food]
Andrew Zimmern's bizarre world of food : brains, bugs,
and blood sausage / Andrew Zimmern. — 1st ed.
p. cm.
ISBN 978-0-385-74003-6 (hc) — ISBN 978-0-385-90820-7 (lib. bdg.)
ISBN 978-0-375-89870-9 (ebook)
[1. International cooking. 2. Cooking (Wild foods). 3. Food habits.
4. Cooking—Humor.] I.Title.
TX725.A1A494 2011
394.1'2—dc22
2011001133

ISBN 978-0-385-74004-3 (trade pbk.)

RL: 4.8

Printed in the United States of America

10 9 8 7 6 5 4 3 2

First Ember Edition 2012

FOR THE KIDS WHOSE PARENTS ARE ALWAYS
TELLING THEM TO PLAY OUTSIDE—
ALWAYS LEAVE THE HOUSE HUNGRY,
AND PACK AN OPEN MIND.

Contents

Introduction—ix

Modern-Day Vikings:
Puffin Hunting in the Land of Fire and Ice—1

The Most Dangerous Game:
How I Almost Lost My Life Tracking Down Samoa's
Elusive Giant Fruit Bat—15

Journey to the Source:
Why the Shortest Distance from Sea to Plate Makes for
Amazing Meals—31

Muddy Waters:
Ugandan Lungfishing Can Be Messy—43

Saving Huatulco:
Free Diving for Octopus—57

Death Match:
Can a Matador Save Madrid's Historic *Tabernas*?—69

Forgotten Foods:
Juicy Cheese Worms Are Making a Comeback!—81

Welcome to a *Wazwan:*
The Meal That Nearly Killed Me—93

Mary's Corner:
The Quest for the Best Laksa in Singapore—105

Simple Foods:
Noodle Houses of Guangzhou—123

Fish Heaven:
Finding Perfection in a Ginza Basement—133

Nature's Candy:
The Achachairu—147

Pleasant Surprises:
A Gallimaufry—155

Some Final Thoughts—177

Acknowledgments—189

Introduction

I am a traveler. I am not a tourist. Occasionally I do touristy things, but I've discovered that diving into a culture mouth-first is my favorite way to explore a new place. It makes me happy. Now I'm reaching out to you, my most important reader. I want you to love to travel, to feel inspired by first-hand accounts of journeys, so you'll go into the heart of the African jungles in search of lost culinary gold. I want you to experience the rush of warm air on your cheek as you exit a tiny plane on the tarmac of a small airfield in South America. I want you to feel your heart race, imagining the adventure of a lifetime that awaits you. I want you to let go.

My parents divorced when I was about six. My mom and I spent summers at the beach house and managed to get to a warm-weather island at least once every year (my mom was writing a book about shells), but my dad was the one who loved to really take off. I traveled a lot with him. At first it was ski weekends in Manchester, Vermont; by the time I was twelve, it was off to Europe. On those trips with my dad, I learned a new approach to spending time in a foreign country.

My dad taught me many things—how to travel, how to write, how to tell a joke and "take the room," how to shop for socks and tie a tie—but most importantly, he taught me how to eat and how to cook. When my dad and I visited London, we spent as much time cruising the aisles at Harrods and exploring Chinatown as we did looking at the British Museum's Elgin Marbles. That's not to say that if you ever find yourself in Rome you should skip the Colosseum or the Forum—those are some of the most awesome sites in the world—but be sure to make time for people-watching in neighborhood cafés as well. That's where you will find the authentic Roman experience.

My dad also taught me that exploring off the beaten path was the best way to experience a country, a culture, and its people. Traveling as far as we could in one day, just for a great meal, was how we rolled. Dad insisted that you don't have to leave the country—or even your area code—to put his traveler's creed into practice. It's easy to forget how much there is to explore right outside your own front door. Every summer, my dad would drive us from our summer home in East Hampton, Long Island, out to Montauk at the island's tip. It was only about twenty miles away, but it felt like the other side of the world. We'd sit on a dock, watching fishing boats unload crates of fresh seafood pulled right out of the Atlantic. My dad and I would hound these crates to the clam bars on Montauk's docks just to eat the freshest food we could—because that's the best it's ever going to taste. Time is the enemy of food. Whenever we could, we'd favor the smaller, local clam bars. That was our summer.

In the winter, we lived to ski. In 1976, we took a family trip to Val d'Isère, France. For the first two days, we woke to six inches of fresh powder under the warm March sun. We were ecstatic. On our third day, it began to snow, and by that afternoon we were forced off the mountain by whiteout conditions. It snowed so heavily for so long that food delivery to the Alpine ski village ceased after a week. By day nine, we were living on sardines and crackers in the hotel lobby. After day ten, the snow finally stopped. The mountain wasn't open for skiing yet, but cars were allowed on the roads. Dad piled everyone into the van and drove all day across France to Paul Bocuse's restaurant in Lyon.

The great French chef Paul Bocuse, one of my heroes, was born on February 11, 1926, making him only a few months older than my father. Critics often remark that without Bocuse, there would be no modern food movement. Bocuse pursued a revolutionary idea that food must be cooked in a way that allows the natural and true flavors of the ingredients to shine through. He believed that quality, technique, improvisation, and fantasy all play roles in defining great cuisine. Each meal you have should be an incredible, fun, and new experience. Savor and enjoy it.

In the 1970s, Bocuse's restaurant was universally regarded as the world's finest. Today, the idea that a chef's food is only as good as his ingredients is no longer novel. Neither is the concept that simple food can be as good as complicated, technique-driven food. Instead of elaborate sauces and ornate presentations, Bocuse relied on the fresh ingredients of

Lyon and provincial France. As I walked through the restaurant, I couldn't stop staring at the fancy chandeliers, white tablecloths, expensive table settings, and ornate decorations. This place was elegant by any standards, and I was intimidated. I crossed my fingers, closed my eyes, and hoped not to break anything. I clearly remember the kitchen help, women in their fifties in traditional long skirts and head coverings, running out into the gardens for the season's first herbs. The aromas were deep and exhilarating, and many dishes were still being served and finished tableside.

I'll never forget the look of shock on my father's face when I spoke and ordered the chef's tasting menu. Dad just shook his head in disbelief—he exuberantly supported my food life, but plunking down a few hundred bucks for his kid's meal didn't make him very happy. I think I had four courses before the entire table was served a balloon of truffle soup *en croûte*, arguably the trendiest dish in the world that year. Bocuse created his famous *soupe aux truffes* for a presidential luncheon at the Elysée Palace in February of 1975, on the day then-president Valéry Giscard d'Estaing was awarded the Legion of Honor. Ever since that day, the soup has been served at the restaurant as *Soupe aux Truffes Noires V.G.E.*— the president's initials. The soup came in an enormous white bowl, crowned with a thin, brittle, buttery dome of puff pastry. I got my first legitimate food high when I tasted that dish, and I knew, at that exact moment in time, that I had to spend my life in the culinary world.

It was a revelation. The *Volaille de Bresse en Vessie "Mère Fillioux"* (Bresse chicken cooked inside a pig's bladder), still one of Bocuse's most famous dishes, was unlike any dish I'd ever experienced. I'd never tasted morel mushrooms like this, or seen sliced truffles slid under a chicken's skin before. I'd never even seen a pig's bladder before! What made the meal complete was meeting the great Bocuse himself, who was kind enough to autograph my menu and who invited me to return. The effect this meal had on me was staggering. I knew I wanted to share stories about food and the people who made it. I knew I needed to see and eat my way around the globe. More importantly, I wanted to understand and experience the culture behind the dish. Knowing the people behind what you eat turns the food into a meal you won't forget.

To this day I remember each culinary journey I took with my dad, and each culinary master, like Paul Bocuse, to whom I was introduced. I believe honesty and authenticity are found at the end of your fork—if you are eating in the right places. Thanks to my dad, I learned to find them.

So to my fellow adventurers: Please be a traveler, not a tourist. Try new things, meet new people, and look beyond what's right in front of you. Those are the keys to understanding this amazing world we live in. I hope you enjoy this book, and I hope you get to walk outside your comfort zone and discover yourself in the process.

Modern-Day Vikings: Puffin Hunting in the Land of Fire and Ice

Iceland looks and feels like no other place on earth. As our plane touched down just outside **Reykjavík,** I was almost convinced we'd landed on the moon. Not surprising, given that NASA astronauts trained in Iceland prior to the first moon landing. In much of the country, the barren, rocky topography looks otherworldly. Iceland, which is roughly the size of Ohio, is a glacial, rocky, moss-covered expanse born from volcanic eruptions. Treeless mountains, sweeping fields of arctic grasses waving out to the horizon, awe-inspiring geysers, raging rivers, spectacular ocean vistas, and therapeutic

> Reykjavík is the world's northernmost capital city and is home to two-thirds of Iceland's total population of about 320,000 people.

hot springs fueled by underwater volcanoes are stunning but make much of the island uninhabitable. Iceland is called the **Land of Fire and Ice,** yet despite its staggering natural beauty, the overwhelming majority of the population lives in the capital city of Reykjavík. Everyone else is a farmer or works in either the thermal energy business (booming) or the greenhouse-gardening industry (emerging).

 Iceland's name implies that the weather is freezing, but that's not the case. Summer temps rarely hit the sixty-degree mark, but the winters are surprisingly mild—the average temperature in January is 32°F.

The country is changing and growing all the time—literally. In 1963, a volcanic explosion just off the southern coast of Iceland created an island that eventually expanded to one square mile in size. This landmass, named Surtsey after Surtur, the Icelandic fire god, grew to this official landmass status in only three and a half years. I was fortunate enough to travel to Surtsey by boat one day. It's a phenomenal thing to see, an island that is as big as it is, that is as new as it is, and freakishly almost exactly as old as I am.

I knew the food in Iceland would be wonderful. As a chef in New York and Minneapolis, I'd always been floored by the quality of the Icelandic lamb, dairy products, and seafood I'd run across from time to time. **Icelandic animals** drink the

The only native land mammal when humans arrived was the arctic fox, which came to the island at the end of the last ice age, walking over the frozen sea. There are no native reptiles or amphibians on the island.

cleanest water on earth, eat the freshest grass, and breathe the purest air. Everything, from the horses to the sheep and cows, is genetically pristine, and the animals are raised not only for their meat but for their milk and cheese products. Skyr, the addictively cheesy yogurt product you see everywhere in Iceland, comes from cows that eat sweet grass for a brief period of time, then silage for most of the year. The cows' diet produces a unique flavor profile that is distinctly their own.

I spent much of my time in Reykjavík, puttering around town and enjoying the beautiful summer weather. **Summer** temperatures climb into the forties during the day, maybe the fifties in the sun.

 Because Iceland is so close to the North Pole, the country experiences midnight sun in the summer. In the winter, expect only four to five hours of daylight.

The food scene in Iceland is vibrant. I was looking forward to my first taste of puffin, those cute little black-and-white birds with big orange beaks. Before you get yourself all worked up about me eating this cute 'n' cuddly creature, consider the fact that only about 320,000 people call Iceland home. The puffin population, on the other hand, runs between 8 and 10 million. Icelanders could eat puffin meat at every meal from now until eternity and they would never make a dent in the region's population. As a matter of fact, they urge people to eat the birds as a point of civic duty because there are just so many of them.

HEADING TO THE SOURCE

But to eat the best puffins, and to hunt them where they live, you need to head south of Reykjavík. There you'll find the Vestmannaeyjar Islands, a cluster of smaller islands that make up one of the region's most famous fishing communities. This area's other claim to fame is the 1973 volcanic eruption on Heimaey, the largest island in the chain. It's Iceland's version of Pompeii, but only a few decades old. Lava flows crushed half the town, and when you see the end results of something that destructive and realize that it happened within your lifetime, it takes your breath away. You see homes buried, and cars half frozen in black, porous rock. Luckily, everyone was able to get off the island in time to save themselves.

Millions of puffins call the Vestmannaeyjar Islands home, and the local restaurateurs take advantage of this ample source of food. The rest of the citizenry are devoted puffin eaters or hunters, or both. Once our six-seat puddle jumper landed on Heimaey, the *Bizarre Foods* production crew and I tried to negotiate our way over to the far side of Vestmannaeyjar, with its simple harbor, occasional spouting orca, seals, and numerous birds. We ended up running into a guy who claimed he could arrange to have us picked up by boat on the far side of the island and taken to an uninhabited area to experience a puffin hunt firsthand. Without hesitation, we piled into our van and headed over.

It's a bright, beautiful summer's day in Iceland, perfect sweatshirt weather. We pass alongside a huge half-moon bay, complete with breathtaking views of the ocean and the outer isles, which include **Surtsey.** We start unloading our gear onto the mile-long black sand beach at Surtsey. There isn't a trace of human imprint as far as you can see. Not a jet contrail in the sky, not a footprint in the sand, not a boat at sea . . . it's just empty and desolate. You know for sure you're at one of the ends of the earth—a feeling I find so satisfying I could have sat on that beach all day.

We Will Rock You: The volcanic island of Surtsey formed during a volcanic eruption that began about 426 feet below the water's surface. It reached the surface on November 14, 1963. The eruption lasted nearly four years—until June 5, 1967! By that time, this newborn island reached its maximum size of one square mile. The land has steadily eroded away in the years since.

We lock our vehicles, thank our new friends, and wait for our guide by a giant piece of driftwood on the beach. After twenty minutes, we see a Zodiac boat putt-putting over to us. It lands on the beach and off steps Pall. He's a modern-day Viking: the kind of guy who would travel alone in a Zodiac, a fourteen-foot flat-bottom rubber boat, across five miles of open ocean from an uninhabited island to pick me up. Hot on Pall's heels is a closed-cabin, twenty-foot cruiser with an inboard engine that will ferry the crew as they capture Pall and me having the "authentic" experience of taking the Zodiac to the island of Alsey, where his family has hunted for years.

As I pile into his boat from the surf side, I feel glad I put on my knee-high rubber boots that morning. The crew has already headed out into the channel on the cruiser, headed toward a giant boulder looming in the distance. I've been in a Zodiac plenty of times, so I plop down on the edge of the craft on the gunwale, just as I did as a little kid puttering around the inner harbors of the South Fork of Long Island. It's the perfect vehicle for flat, calm water. Easy in, easy out. But today Pall instructs me to sit down on the floor of the boat itself, explaining that's how it's done in Iceland. I'm all confused—*What do you mean, sit on the flat bottom? In the water, no less?* And in his stern, Vikingly way, he says it again: Sit on the flat bottom. Next, he instructs me to wrap my arms around the ropes attached to the gunwales. *What do you mean, wrap my arms around the ropes?* He explains that I have to hang on tight unless I want to get thrown out of the boat. It is then that I begin to get a faint idea of what the afternoon will hold for me. He turns toward me, sees the look on my face, and a huge grin spreads across his. "Today will be a great test of your manhood," he tells me. And he goes back to staring out at the horizon as he guides the boat out of the quiet water and into the rolling seas.

When you're in a fourteen-foot flat-bottom Zodiac in rolling waves, maybe about eight or ten feet high, it's like being stuck on the longest roller-coaster ride of your life. No life preservers. No radio. Just me and Pall the Viking, cranking down the engine as hard as it could go in this little rubber dinghy. Oh, and in case you forgot, we're in Iceland. The water is just a degree above freezing. We are miles and miles from civilization as the crow files, at least ten miles from the nearest town. If you fall into that water, you're a goner. You can't survive; it's just too cold. I say a prayer in my head.

Out of nowhere, an entire pod of killer whales pops up next to us. All those friendly, SeaWorld-inspired killer whale images go right out the window when you see this thirty-foot monstrosity cresting the waves adjacent to your little boat. I am sitting so low in that boat that I am almost eye level with the water. The killer whales are right there. The immediacy of the situation is oddly thrilling. The fear that is on my face becomes more and more evident to Pall, who just keeps smiling at me.

We finally arrive at our destination after about half an hour at sea, up the side of a wave and down the other side, repeat. The island looks like a giant cylinder of granite rising straight up out of the water—topped with a grassy 1980s haircut. As we get closer, I can see a wooden cabin built on stilts on the side of the cliff. And I think I can see Pall's family waving at us.

It turns out that every year in puffin-hunting season,

which is about two weeks long, three generations of Pall's family—father, brothers, kids—head to Alsey and spend a few days hunting as many puffin as they can. I'm talking thousands of birds. They've done it every year since Pall's father, now the patriarch of the family, was a kid. This is their ancestral tradition.

We cruise into some softer **water** about a quarter mile offshore and idle beside a two-inch-thick wire coming from the house and disappearing into the water beside us. I learn

 Puffins are excellent underwater swimmers and are known to dive to depths of 180 feet.

that the only way to unload the gear is by means of a pulley system. Several years earlier, the family sank a giant anchor into the water, attached a wire cable about five hundred feet off the cliff, and then pulled the wire up to the house, securing it with block and tackle to a landing about fifty feet below the house's platform. They lower the tackle, hooked up with a giant cargo net, toward the water and we load up all our gear from the two boats. I watch the net disappear as six or seven guys yank all the equipment to the top of the hill.

OUR AEROBATIC CLIMB

Here's the method of hopping onto Alsey: You run the little Zodiac boat at top speed, straight toward the rock face of the cliff. A split second before the boat's nose smashes into the granite wall, Pall guns it into reverse. The boat freezes and you jump out at the last possible moment of sweet inertia, grasping, struggling to clutch the flimsy climbing rope dangling from some pitons high atop the cliff. As the boat pulls away, you hold yourself there, balance your feet on the slippery wet rocks, and essentially pull yourself up, Batman Bat-rope style. Foot over foot, hand over hand, while (if you are lucky) kind people who've arrived before you attempt to pull on the rope to make it a little easier for you. In comparison, getting back is a piece of cake. You just hang on to the rope, and when the boat comes in, you let go and fall (indelicately, I might add) into the Zodiac with a big thud. But leaping out of that boat onto the rock wall, aiming for this little piece of climbing rope about the width of your pinky, is one of those experiences that I will never forget. A literal leap of faith.

I knew that this great test of my manhood was not going to get any easier. Fortunately, Pall was a great coach, and he talked us through the whole thing. Our crew was wet, bruised, and scraped, but without Pall's expertise, we didn't have a prayer. Our success was directly related to the skill set of our leader, and he had gotten us all on the **island.**

> From Poop to Root? Surtsey was declared a nature reserve in 1965, and island access is restricted to a few scientists. All visitors are subject to search to ensure that no foreign species or seeds are accidentally introduced into the ecosystem. They take this very seriously—in fact, when an improperly handled human defecation resulted in a tomato plant's taking root, the plant was promptly destroyed.

We reconned on the top of the granite cliff and climbed our way to the crest of the upper hillside, walking carefully along the cut-in path to the stone path at the highest part of the bluff, then up and over the last ridge to the family's hunting cabin. We walked about a quarter mile from the landing point to the house itself, where we changed into our puffin-hunting clothes, sturdier shoes, tough mackinaw jackets, hats, and hunting equipment.

HOW TO HUNT A PUFFIN

Now, **puffin hunting** is done in a very specific way. You hide yourself in the rocks, holding on to a long and extremely unwieldy, twenty-foot-long, thick wooden pole that weighs at least forty pounds. At the end of the pole they've attached a big net. You time it precisely. When you see a puffin flitting past you, you swing this massively heavy net at it and attempt to guide the net toward the puffin's flight path. It's an ungainly process; the stick is so heavy and awkwardly long, it's like netting extremely speedy butterflies but on a much larger scale. The birds are so dumb that they don't really know how to move out of the way. Once you get a feel for how the puffins react, you can be very successful, starting your long, slow, arcing swing, aiming at an imagined point where the bird's flight path will intersect with the future position of your net.

> Iceland is home to one of the world's largest colonies of puffins. Over half of the world population of the Atlantic puffin breeds in Iceland.

When you see someone with a lot of experience do it, it almost seems like they can will the bird into the basket. Pall's eight-year-old nephew netted about four of them while I was just getting comfy in my spider hole burrow. Pall's youngest son nabbed an additional two or three birds. His twelve-year-old son did the same, as did Pall and his brother. In an hour and a half, I netted one. It is as easy as shooting fish in a barrel, but only if you know how the puffins fly and aren't completely preoccupied by the thought of slipping and plummeting to your untimely demise. I almost fell off the hill the couple of times I summoned the courage to stand and swing my pole. The hill is nearly vertical, pitted with **puffin nests** that are covered in thick matted grass, so you can't see the rocks and ridges. That, in addition to the steepness, makes the terrain impracticable for anything other than squatting on it.

> Puffins don't build nests like most birds. Instead, they create soft underground burrows. The burrows are usually about two feet in length. Unless it is destroyed, puffins often use the same burrow for years. In one study, scientists discovered that one puffin returned to the same burrow for over thirty years!

There was a charming aspect to it. If you leaned out over the edge of the cliff just enough and looked down, you could see all the wild seals basking on the rocks, swimming to and fro and making cute seal noises. You could see the orcas blasting through their blowholes, rounding up krill, and all the seabirds diving into the water for their evening meal. It was glorious.

As the weather began to cool off, we took the birds out of the net, gently put them out of their misery, and breasted them out. Puffin meat looks a lot like that of wild bufflehead duck: very dark and very purplish, with a small breast size. I'm accustomed to eating wild ducks and I've sampled sea ducks, which have some of the worst-tasting meat in the whole world—chewy, fishy, dry, and oppressively oily. I was expecting puffin to fall into this category, but the grilled puffin I ate on the deck outside the Alsey cabin was one of the most delicious meats ever to pass my lips. It tasted like a delicately mild, finely grained piece of elk (or ostrich, even) that had been waved over a pot of clam juice. The salty and sealife-intense diet these puffins have makes them naturally seasoned, in a sense. Not grilling them past medium-rare helps. Pall and the lads sprinkled the meat with salt, pepper, and a dash of their favorite grilling spice from the local supermarket and we devoured the entire platter before we even got inside the cabin.

Our hosts served up some smoked puffin once we got indoors. Smoked puffin is the most popular preparation you will find in Icelandic restaurants, mostly because it is so stable and can sit in the fridge for weeks at a time without degrading in quality. We sliced it paper thin, pairing the meat with sweet Galia melon. Here is yet another oddity of Iceland: they have no growing season. Sure, they have some hydroponic stuff that is coming out of local greenhouses, but not much of it. A bag of carrots in Iceland costs ten dollars, but a pound of lamb or a pound of crayfish costs next to nothing. It's the exact reverse of the way it is in the rest of the world. Imagine a culture with plentiful meat and fish that are very cheap, but where all the vegetables are very expensive because they're shipped in from other places.

> 🧳 Puffins usually keep the same mates for life.

BACK TO SEA WE GO

The puddle jumper we'd chartered was leaving the air-port in a few hours, and we knew that if we didn't get off the island fast, we'd miss the flight. We said our good-byes, scam-pered down the path we'd arrived on, climbed down the ropes, and dropped ourselves into the Zodiac, falling onto the wet bottom. We ferried the crew out to the big boat and took our equipment off the zip line as Pall's brother and his kids sent it hurtling down from the house platform. Before heading back to the cruiser to drop me off, Pall took the Zodiac around to some of the caves where we had spotted some seals. He held the boat steady while huge waves broke on the rocks just in front of us, and I got a chance to stand a foot or so away from the wild seals before he took me back to the crew on the cabin cruiser, where we continued back to the main island.

Pall orchestrated a nice send-off for us, popping wheelies with his Zodiac against these giant rolling waves as his whole family gave us the Alsey cheer from the deck. They shouted, "Alsey, Alsey, ah-ah-ah!" as we putt-putted off into the sun-set, killer whales trailing us, cresting the surface of the water around our boat. It was probably the most exhilarating day of travel that I'd ever had in my life up to that point, the charm of the simplicity of another way of life quickly quashed by the modern-day fact that we had to race to catch a plane. We arrived at the harbor in the darkness and had to hijack several locals, begging them for a lift to the airstrip to catch our plane, almost leaving our guide, Svein, behind in the chaos.

The sense of accomplishment I felt after that day was incredible. The food was singularly fantastic; I have never had any eating experience like that. It's the type of eating that, as a collector of these moments in life, I find unique. It's hard to measure it against anything else. I have yet to bump into any other group of people in my world who have hunted wild puffins and eaten them. I know there are some out there, non-Icelanders, but we are a rather small bunch.

There is a postscript to this adventure. The day after our excursion, the cabin cruiser that took us home hit a rock and sank. Due to all the volcanic activity in the area, the ocean floor is always in flux. Giant rocks can form quickly, rendering depth charts useless. It's ironic that during the time I felt most secure, I was probably most in danger.

The Most Dangerous Game: How I Almost Lost My Life Tracking Down Samoa's Elusive Giant Fruit Bat

Traveling from American Samoa to Samoa is a shot in the arm. Yes, it's the same part of the world, and to many observers there may not seem to be any difference between the two, but nothing could be further from the case. American Samoa is an overgrown military installation of an island with a modicum of beach tourism. Land in American Samoa and you come face-to-face with the least appealing aspects of America's greatest contribution to world culture: the miles-long strip of fast-food places and motels.

Just a white-knuckled puddle jump away lies the stunningly beautiful, relatively unvisited **islands of Samoa.** A multi-island chain of breathtaking atolls, Samoa just might be the last great unspoiled deep-Pacific country. I was beaming

> The islands of Samoa are made up of solidified lava produced by volcanoes, but only one island, Savaii, is still volcanically active. The last eruption occurred in 1911.

as our six-seater twin-prop departed American Samoa, destined for its much better-looking sibling.

It takes only a half hour or so to head into Upolu, the most **populated** of the Samoa Islands chain. We hopped into our van after a gentle landing and were off to the Aggie Grey's Hotel in the heart of Apia, the capital city of Samoa. This Samoa is the one in your dreams: quaint city streets speckled with old colonial-style bungalows surrounded by brilliant tropical gardens, interspersed with marine shops and small local banks. Welcome to Samoa.

> The islands of Samoa are home to roughly 188,000 people. There are 362 *nu'u* (villages) found throughout the islands, with a total of eighteen thousand *matai* (chiefs).

> *Fale,* Sweet *Fale:* Enjoy alone time? Then a traditional Samoan home is probably not for you. Samoan *fales* (houses) traditionally don't have walls. They use blinds made of coconut palm fronds during the night or in bad weather.

We rounded the main harbor, snug with luxury sailcraft, industrial rust buckets, and professionally outfitted fishing boats all bobbing in the early-morning sun. We pulled into the turnaround of Aggie's and fled the van for the friendly confines of the elegant lobby replete with a cozy coffee and tea lounge and a kitschy, open-air dining room with a few ukulele players, a guitarist, and piano player pounding out

Polynesian-style music at all three meal periods for **guests** willing to endure the agony. Aggie Grey's is the Samoa of William Somerset Maugham and Robert Louis Stevenson,

---

¶¶¶ Mind your manners and your feet! It's customary to remove your shoes before entering a *fale*. Once inside, it's best to sit pretzel-style (with your legs crossed), kneel with your feet tucked under, or cover your feet with a sarong. Pointing the bottoms of your feet at others is considered rude.

---

an ancient hotel with luxurious gardens and a pedigree that most hotels would kill for. Ignore the fact that services like Internet or phones are offered but don't function, and focus on the fact that other hotels like Aggie Grey's simply don't exist anymore; they belong to an era when traveling to Samoa meant staying for several months until the next tramp steamer left the harbor. Of course, traveling is different now.

TO THE VILLAGE WE GO

We unpacked and headed out to shoot the little village of Tafagamanu, where the local government, in partnership with several nature conservancies, had established an underwater protection site for the study and propagation of the giant Pacific clam, a behemoth of a mollusk that can grow to the size of a Volkswagen Beetle if it has the time. Before we crept into the water to shoot our story, we met with the local **villagers** and their *matai*, or chieftain. He greeted us at the large open *fale* that the tribe gathers in for important meetings and served us some **homemade cocoa,** and we made small talk for a few hours, much to the upset of my field producer, who was anxious to start shooting.

Avoid walking through villages during the evening prayer curfew (usually between six p.m. and seven p.m.). This usually lasts for ten to twenty minutes and is often marked at the beginning and end by the ringing of a bell or the blowing of a conch shell.

The staple products of Samoa are copra (dried coconut meat), cacao bean (for chocolate), and bananas. The annual production of both bananas and copra has been in the range of thirteen thousand to fifteen thousand metric tons—that's equal to the weight of about 1,180 school buses!

In Samoa, every shoot each day begins with a business deal. Every story is shot in a different location, and the locations are controlled in every sense of the word by the local tribes, who received the islands back from the New Zealand government several decades ago. The Kiwis know how to leave a country, and after their colonial experiment tanked they ceded the country back to the tribes themselves, hundreds of them, so while there is a government in Samoa, the tribes and extended families own the land and the waterfront—another reason why there is so little development here. But to shoot each day means sitting and getting the blessing of the local people who control your every move.

THE FOOD OF THE LAND
AND WHAT THE LOCALS REALLY EAT

The Samoans are addicted to the cheapest processed meats in the world. Canned hash, Dinty Moore stew, SPAM—they can't get enough of it, so doing business in Samoa required a constant shuttling back and forth to the local supermarket with Fitu, our fixer, piling can after can of the vile stuff into the back of the minivan. Irony of ironies: As we strolled around the **island,** dosing out canned meat products with casualness, we ate very well. Oranges, grapefruit, dozens of banana varietals, and every other tropical fruit you can imagine grow extremely well here and can be had for pennies. Tuna is sold on the side of the roads for about a dollar a pound, and that's the rip-off tourist rate.

> Up until 1993, the taro root crop, traditionally Samoa's largest export, generated more than half of the country's export revenue. But a vicious fungus destroyed the plants, and since 1994 taro exports account for less than one percent of export revenue.

Every day, hundreds of local fishermen head out into the surf in teeny little canoes fitted with an outrigger to pull in the local yellowfin and blackfin tuna on hand lines. You heard me right. Sometimes as small as a few pounds, often as big as a man, the local tuna are traded around the island like a commodity. You can pay bills with tuna, sell it from the side of the road, deliver it to the back door of a restaurant kitchen by foot, or bring it to the local market. It's a tuna economy here unlike anything I have ever seen before or since.

We awoke the next day and headed out to sea, traveling four hours into the South Pacific Ocean, where the big tuna run fast and thick. Deep-sea fishing is a passion of mine, and buckled into the fighting chair with several monsters hooked on the multiple lines we were running was thrilling in the extreme. Reeling a huge tuna into the boat is a challenge, but the motivation provided by the groan of the outriggers and the movement of the crew—sweeping fish out of the water with their gaffs, lashing the outrigger lines to my rod, and starting the whole process over and over until the coolers were full and we headed back to shore—made for an easy day of work.

Of course, eating the catch is what it's all about, and while clichéd, slicing and scarfing huge chunks of fresh tuna, raw, under the high, hot Pacific sun is about as good a food day as one can have. The captain came down from the uppermost deck to show me the joys of true poke, mixing tuna with lime juice and coconut, cracking open the eyes of the fish and filling them with lime juice and soy sauce, and arguing over who would eat the still-beating hearts of the fish. We even got to try palolo, a rarity even in this part of the world, where these tiny little coral worms are eaten when they swim out of the coral to propagate twice a year. Sautéed in butter, they look like blue cream cheese and taste like rotten eggs mixed with anchovies, but spread on toast they are an addictive snack.

We woke at dawn and traveled to the southeastern coast, to the little town of Aleipata. On the horizon, as gazed at from the town's public dock, lies a small cluster of uninhabited volcanic islands, the largest one being Nu'utele, which is known for its pristine flora and fauna and is home to a rare and delicious breed of giant fruit bats. Five-pound giant fruit bats, often referred to as flying foxes. Large, furry, brown-and-black bats. Yum-o!

THE "TINY TIN CAN" BOAT

It was on the beaches of Aleipata that I met the man who would eventually save my life. Afele Faiilagi, an environmental scientist with the Samoan Forestry Department.

Afele commissioned a boat to take us out to Nu'utele. I use the term "boat" loosely; it was more like a tiny tin can, an ancient pontoon boat with an ailing 1960s Evinrude outboard on the back end, fastened to the transom with picture-hanging wire. We piled on the crew, our guests, and five hundred pounds of gear, pulling off from the dock in a warm and light morning rain. As soon as our voyage was under way, I got the feeling that the humble amount we had offered up for our five-mile voyage was probably more money than our anxious captain and mate had seen in months. It occurred to me that they probably said yes to the job not thinking of whether or not they could get us there safely with all our gear, or whether their boat was up to the task based on the day's weather forecast, but instead had seen the visions of sugarplums that our currency represented. On the road, the small sum of money we see as only a token payment is often a gargantuan amount to the person staring down at it. So the person takes risks—stupid, unfathomable risks.

Well, the bay outside the harbor dock is flat as glass, it's ten feet deep, and the boat is gliding out of her slip. We get out in the middle of the channel, and it's only five miles across to Nu'utele, when all of a sudden, about a half mile from shore, we are in ocean several hundred feet deep in fourteen- or fifteen-foot seas, big rolling waves coming under the pontoons, and this little tin can of a boat is being pushed sideways. I'm petrified. I look around: There are no life jackets . . . there is no radio. The vintage forty-horsepower engine that is trying to push us over to this island is failing miserably. The guy who's driving the boat looks like the kid who carried my bags at the hotel but doesn't seem half as confident about making it to his destination, and he's got this worried look on his face. And all of a sudden, what had started as a *Wow, this is sort of scary and thrilling* thing became scarier and scarier and scarier as the waves got bigger and the boat began to get pushed around more and more.

The overcast sky swirled around us, the wind rose and fell, and my producer started singing the theme from *Gilligan's Island*: "Just sit right back and you'll hear a tale, a tale of a fateful trip that started from this tropic port aboard this tiny ship." Chris volunteered that when he's really scared he does that to calm himself, and I looked over at Joel, one of our videographers, and he looked really scared. I felt really scared, and I realized in a flash that we all felt somewhat doomed, in the middle of the ocean, on the boat ride to nowhere.

HOPE ON THE HORIZON

After much nail biting and hair pulling, we finally got within the calm natural harbor of Nu'utele. The sun came out, the waters were tranquil, and all we had to do was navigate through a maze of car- and bus-size rocks in this bay and try to beach the boat on the rocky shoreline. We did, and ran two lines, one to either end of the pontoon boat, then up and around the massive palm trees that stand vigil on the shoreline. For about an hour, in waist-deep water, we ferried all our gear off the boat and made a temporary base camp in the trees.

Afele does a fantastic job helping us get situated under a little lean-to that is hidden in a small glade about a hundred yards up and off the beach. When you reach it, dense tropical rain forest is all around you and at times you can't see five feet in front of your face, so the clearing and the corrugated steel topper on the old tent poles make a nice resting spot. No one lives on the island, but a lot of visiting biologists and other scientists venture out to Nu'utele to aid their studies, and the shelter is a constant on everyone's trip here.

TO THE TOP OF THE MOUNTAIN

Afele shows me water vines and edible snakes. We hack apart rotting palms looking for bugs and grubs, and he shows me sleeping snakes. We hack away with our machetes almost every few steps, looking for coconut grubs, and can't find any. In fact, we spend all morning looking for coconut grubs—after all, that was supposed to be an important part of our story—and we finally get to the point where Afele, exhausted and dejected but keeping it all close to the vest, suggests we start to climb the mountain. There is only one mountain, rising up out of the center of this island—and remember, the whole island chain is essentially volcanic, so the general topographic vibe is like you are walking on a giant inverted ice cream cone squished on top of a small pancake, and since Nu'utele's soil is clay-based on this side of the mountain, we are having an incredibly tough time making any headway.

The rainstorm that came through last night and earlier in the morning keeps threatening rain again, but it burns off every time the sun appears ready to peek out. It's a bright but cloudy afternoon, and the ground is so wet and slick that you can't get any traction on it even with sturdy hiking shoes.

The slopes are almost a full forty-five degrees steep, but it feels worse as we slip and slide, and one by one our crew gives up—something that has never happened before—forced to turn back, unable to climb this mountain.

Everybody is carrying tripods, cameras, and equipment, so it takes us a while on the narrow path we are cutting to actually turn around. Afele sends us back on our own as he continues to scamper up the incline in his flip-flops, cruising up the mountain in pursuit of a few weevils or grubs, and we go back to the little shelter to wait for the arrival of the second group of intrepid locals coming to meet us for part two of our island experience.

By this time, the mood is sour. Half the day is gone and we still have no story in the can, Afele is up on the mountain and we don't know what he is doing or when he is coming back, and we roll into our base camp to meet the Samoan Bat-Hunting Club, coming to take us on a bat hunt.

WITH HELP FROM THE HUNTING CLUB

With a name like that, the Samoan Bat-Hunting Club sounds very elegant. But it was a group of just eight **guys,** all of whom really dug going out into the woods and blasting away at bats with their guns. Also, the members were divided

> Extreme Ink: Samoans are known for their intricate and significant tattoos. Getting the traditional male tattoo, called *pe'a,* is a very painful ordeal. The tattoo is etched onto the skin with handmade tools made of bones, tusks, turtle shells, and wood. Once completed, the *pe'a* covers the entire body—from the navel to just below the knee!

into two cliques. The first was made up of their self-appointed leader, named Paul, and the four guys who were his pals. The other clique was made up of the three guys who didn't give a whit what Paul said or did. They had some kind of independent life outside of the hunting club—one was a cop, the others local laborers—but all absent allegiance to the loud-mouth who ran the show.

You can't really start hunting bats until the sun starts setting, so we had quite an amount of time on our hands while we were waiting for Afele to return to camp. We enjoyed talking to some of these guys, so we began to shoot B-roll and do some of the little nuts-and-bolts TV business that we needed to capture before the big scene, getting a safety lesson on the weapons, doing the meet and greet, and so on. We almost lose our lives in the water getting turned sideways going out to Nu'utele, and now the boat breaks free of its moorings and we almost get stranded out there. Sometimes I tell myself that what we are doing is just a little too goofy and dangerous, and at that point in the evolution of the show we had no satellite phone with us and no way to get off the island if something really bad happened. The idea of being marooned was not appealing.

THE GIANT FLYING FRUIT BAT

Eventually, we get the boat squared away. The dust begins to settle and the magic begins to happen. The weather has cleared up, the humidity has dropped, the ruckus on this abandoned island is settling down, shadows begin to appear on the mountaintop, and we stand vigil underneath the breadfruit trees and wait for the bats. Well, the bats on Nuʻutele are not very far-ranging—and when I say bats, you're probably thinking of something flitting around the backyard in Connecticut on warm summer nights, a pest that weighs a couple of ounces and occasionally flies by accident into your living room, and you fetch a tennis racket and shoo it out the kitchen door. No, these fruit bats tip the scales at five pounds—giant tropical fruit bats, also known as flying foxes because they are so ferocious-looking, supersized, and furry. This bat has as much relation to a bat in your backyard as my sitting in your garage has to my being your car. It is an awesome sight to see hundreds of these things pinwheeling in the sky, circling down, down, down from the mountaintop caves they live in toward the breadfruit trees dotting the shoreline.

All these bats do is sleep, poop, and eat ripe breadfruit. These animals are a rarity in the animal kingdom in that once you do kill them and begin preparing them for eating, you don't even have to clean them in the traditional butchery sense of the word. Even the stuff in the intestinal tract is good to eat, and the natives eat all of it. These animals are not purged or bled after harvesting; these things (with a six-foot wingspan) are simply held by two men over an open fire to be scraped of their fur and roasted whole, simply scored with a little X mark in the chest so they cook evenly. These animals are supremely clean. All they eat and digest is breadfruit, and since that's all that's in their system, their gastrointestinal acids and enzymes are relatively mild, so you can eat the whole animal with impunity. That's quite an unusual thing to partake of in the food world, an animal so clean and limited in range that you can eat every edible portion without cleaning it.

So we position ourselves in the jungle, spread out in a line in the little clearing between a couple of breadfruit trees heavy with ripe fruit, and begin shooting bat after bat after bat as they soar into the trees, dropping four or five fairly quickly. The cop who is a member of the shooting team makes one of the most miraculous hunting shots I've ever seen in my life. Out of the corner of his eye—I don't know how he could see it given that it was pitch black at night— he sees something fluttering about eye height and he drops it on the fly in the dark about forty feet out. Turned out it was a true wild chicken, taken on the wing.

CAVEMAN DINING

We've got the five or six coconut grubs that Afele had scrounged up; we've got a half-dozen bats and a wild chicken. Things are looking up. We head back to our shelter, burn a couple of coconut husks, and start a **roaring fire.** We clean the bats one by one, stretching them across the fire, scraping off their fur as they scorch, and scoring them across the chest.

Want to nuke your meal in the microwave? Forget about it! At a Samoan *fale,* food is prepared outdoors in an *umu*—a pit dug in the ground and filled with hot stones. Fish, pork, and chicken are often cooked in the *umu,* wrapped in banana leaves or placed in halved coconut shells. Once the stones are red hot and the food is placed on them, banana leaves are placed all over the food to seal in the heat. Two hours later, the *umu* is opened and the piping hot food is served. Yum!

We toss the bats on the coals and squat on our haunches, turning them every few minutes, getting hungrier and hungrier, just like at a Sunday-afternoon weenie roast back home. Almost. Holding a bat whose wingspan is five or six feet from tip to tip, stretching one of these critters over an open fire to singe the fur, scraping off the hairy soot, taking a sharp knife and putting an X mark in its chest, opening the body up so it cooks evenly, watching the guts start to puff out as the meat cooks—well, this is really caveman-style eating, to say the least.

Dining on bats in the great outdoors is a very greasy, smelly affair. You chew and tear as you go, the meat and sinew are fairly tough, and the process is slow and sloppy. We rinse ourselves off with buckets of rainwater, and finally we cut the cameras and the lights and pack up all of our stuff. By this time it's about eleven at night and we are exhausted. We head down to the boat and load all our gear. The shooting club guys have gone off as quickly and mysteriously as they arrived, piling into their boat and heading off to Upolu. We start to putt-putt out of the protected harbor beach area on Nu'utele, only to find that with the tide up you can't see all the giant rocks that were so easy to cruise around and through on the way in.

OUR BATTLE WITH MOTHER NATURE

The "crew" of our little tin dinghy have no idea how to get us out of the bay on Nu'utele, and we discover that in fact they have never left the island after dark. We also come to learn, as we are going back and forth performing K-turns in vain attempts to get out into deeper water, that the crew are not sure how to get us across the channel to where the water is hundreds of feet deep. The water we are heading into is so deep that the swift, angry current creates huge waves between the big island of Upolu and the little island of Nuʻutele just off the coast. The speed of the current in this deep V-shaped trough is scary fast, but eventually we get turned toward Upolu in our little vessel more suited to flat, lazy lakes than to the deep South Pacific.

We get about a half mile off the island, and despite the whistling winds and boiling seas, we can hear the sickening scrape of metal against rock. I will tell you there is no worse feeling in the world than standing in a tin can of a boat with no radio and no life preservers, with a bunch of crazed, unseaworthy crew members.

That scrape of boat against rock meant just one thing and we all knew it, and if we hadn't already gashed open one of the pontoons and the boat was going to sink, we were about to. I considered my options quickly and figured out that if the boat started to sink, we could all make the decision to try to swim to shore for ourselves. What was really scary was that the boat was stuck on top of one of these rocks, and because the rocks were close to the surface they allowed rollers from out in the open ocean to become breaking waves. The waves threatened to swamp the boat after flipping it over, which would have been disastrous. That's the type of scenario where people really get hurt and—we all realized at the same time—panic begins to set in.

Everyone is screaming at each other. The guides and the crew are all vainly grabbing at poles that are stowed on the boat to push us off the rock. Two, three, or four waves in a row almost loose us from atop this rock, but in doing so also almost flip us over each time they swirl and crash around the rock and our craft. Out of nowhere, Afele tosses aside his T-shirt and dives into the water in the middle of the ocean, swims around to the edge of the boat where the rock has snagged us, waits for the next wave to come, puts his little flip-flop feet up on the rock, and pushes the boat off from where we had been wedged as the water crashes over him. He nonchalantly hops back onto the boat, grabs the handle of the little outboard engine from our incompetent captain, and motors us off into the deeper channel.

Out in the deep water the rollers were surprisingly big and soft and the wind was nil. We flitted and threaded between the waves all the way back to the safe harbor on the big island of Upolu that we had embarked from fourteen hours earlier, capping one of the most energizing and thrilling evenings of my life. On this night I had thought on several occasions that I might lose my life, and it turned out to be one of those great days, a day that you look back on and say, yeah, I did that, making my bat meal taste all the sweeter each time I thought about it.

Journey to the Source: Why the Shortest Distance from Sea to Plate Makes for Amazing Meals

Time is the enemy of great-tasting food, and so I believe in pursuing food at its source. I want whatever is freshest on my plate. I want lobster that goes from the sea straight into a pot of boiling water. I want shrimp that's pulled directly from a fisherman's raft through a rope-and-pulley system out of the bay and right into a kitchen. Those ingredients can't compare to the sitting-around-the-food-locker stuff from a nameless, faceless mainline supplier. God knows how long those edibles spend in the depths of some industrial freezer, how far they've traveled to get to your plate, and how they've been handled along the way. With the exception of a few ingredients—wine and cheese come to mind—the idea that freshness counts is as old as the hills. Traveling in its purest form allows you to gain unbridled access to foods at their source.

Growing up in New York City, we rarely ate food at its freshest. You don't find shrimp in the Hudson River. There was **lobster** once, but 125 years ago they were overfished out of the tidal estuaries around the island of Manhattan.

> **Freaky Fact:** Lobsters can regenerate legs, claws, and antennae. In fact, they can amputate their own claws and legs as a defensive tactic to escape predators.

Every summer, my dad would drive me out to Montauk, on Long Island. We'd sit at the dock, watching fishing boats unload crates of fresh seafood right out of the Atlantic. Like paparazzi hot on some young starlet's trail, we would hound those crates to the clam bars on Montauk's docks just to eat the freshest catch.

There was one big tourist restaurant, called Gosman's, on the waterfront at Montauk. They had pretty fresh stuff, but their **lobsters** were held in aerated, ocean-water tanks to keep them alive. Standard ops then and now for larger commercial seafood restaurants. Minute by minute, day by day, the meat would break down. The lobsters became less

> **Scream Queen:** Word on the street says lobsters scream when placed in boiling hot water. However, that's not exactly the case. The Lobster Institute, based in Maine, states that a lobster's nervous system is very simple. In fact, a lobster doesn't even have a brain. A lobster would require a more complex nervous system in order to perceive pain. It also has no vocal cords. So what is that high-pitched squeal coming from the stove? Most likely, it's steam escaping from underneath the lobster's shell.

flavorful, less briny, less saline, less intense the longer they sat in the tanks. Time is the enemy of food, even when the food is still alive.

THE FRESHEST LOBSTER YOU WILL FIND

Now in his eighties, my father is still as tenacious a traveler as anyone. About five years ago, he moved to Portland, Maine. If you hold a map of Maine under a magnifying glass, you'll see that the coastline looks like a thousand little fingers pointing into the Atlantic Ocean. In some areas, these peninsulas are protected from the brunt of the Atlantic storms by islands, and this creates quiet waters perfect for fishing and lobstering. I don't care how many times you've dined at fancy seafood restaurants in Chicago or New York: Until you've had lobster fresh from the cold waters of Maine, you really haven't had live lobster.

The very first time I visited Dad in Portland, he insisted we drive up to the Five Islands Lobster Company for what he felt was the best lobster roll in the state. Five Islands is one of those rare food finds, if you can find it at all. You drive about forty-five minutes north of Portland on I-295, make a right, and head east on US-1. You begin to head east down county road 127, onto the paved road, turn left onto a dirt road, and you'll drive right up to the eighty-year-old, barn-like wooden structures, where you can park and get some fresh air. Just look for the signs saying "Five Islands Lobster Company"—you can't miss it. The family still goes out every day and lobsters. That's their main business. You can sit and watch their boats coming in with crates and crates of lobsters, some headed off to the world's finest restaurants and fish shops. However, the family keeps the best stuff for themselves. Steamer clams, haddock, hake, clams on the half shell, local shrimp, oysters, or their famous lobster: It's all fresh and delicious, and they're cooking it on the spot.

The thing that sets Five Islands apart from the rest of the clam shacks I love is not just that the lobster marches straight from the traps to the kitchen. This family takes their product so seriously that they don't want a giant food-service truck unloading on their dock. They could doctor up a decent tartar sauce from a jar, but they don't. They make their own from scratch, and the quality of their lobster rolls and hand-dusted fried clams is well beyond that of their competitors. The Five Islands lobster roll is a singular experience. You don't even notice the mayonnaise coating the meat, even as you put the overstuffed toasted hot-dog bun into your gaping maw. I am usually good for two, plus a little side order of clams.

WHICH KIND IS BETTER?

Now, there are two schools of thought when it comes to lobster rolls in Maine. The first kind of lobster roll, which you'll find at Five Islands, contains a lobster salad coated with a gossamer-thin gloss of mayonnaise, plus salt and pepper. The other kind, which they do best at Red's in Wiscasset, is simply a warm lobster plucked from its shell and put into a toasted bun and drizzled with melted butter. Mainers will argue at length about which version is the authentic Maine lobster roll, but frankly the point is moot. They both rock.

Just like Maine with its lobster rolls, every country, state, or city has its own hidden gems if you know where to look. It's the same in the Philippines. It's mind-boggling to realize that, in a country with close to 100 million inhabitants, few locals have ever traveled to the southern island state of Palawan. With its sky-blue water, fresh produce, and incredible seafood, Palawan seems like heaven on earth—yet this picturesque locale is without a doubt the island less traveled. Simply put, people don't know it exists. Sitting to the north and east of Palawan's Puerto Princesa, Boracay is the siren of the Philippine Islands, luring in tourists with its famous diving, snorkeling, and beautiful beaches.

Gross Lobster Facts

These crustaceans may be an expensive delicacy, but that doesn't mean they're free of weird (and sometimes nasty) factoids.

~Lobster blood is clear, but it turns an opaque white when cooked. Best part? Though it doesn't have much flavor, you can eat it!

~Ever seen the mushy green stuff in a lobster's body cavity? It's known as the tomalley, and it fulfills the functions of both the liver and the pancreas. Many people consider tomalley to be a delicacy, while others avoid it altogether. I think it's delicious.

~Lobsters need to shed their shells, or molt, as they grow. They increase in size by about 20 percent at every molt. A lobster averages four or five molts per year until it has reached full size. After molting, lobsters often devour their own recently vacated shells!

Boracay may have great underwater activities, but you're not going to find a lot in the way of honest and authentic culture there, especially when compared to the rest of

Palawan. For me, going to the last stop on the subway means actually going where the locals go, eating what the locals eat, and doing it in a place that still maintains its sense of local relevance. In a world that is becoming flatter every day, where globalization has killed so much indigenous food culture, these end-of-the-line locales are the last unspoiled destinations for travelers craving a unique experience.

Puerto Princesa houses a few decent restaurants, and I did eat some superb meals at Kinabuchs. But craving a one-of-a-kind experience, I headed with the crew into the most remote section of the mangrove forests on the outskirts of the city and found the Badjao Seafront Restaurant. Mangroves are like nature's version of the medieval walled city. These weedlike trees grow very quickly, and the growth becomes almost impenetrable within a few years. They densely populate Southeast Asia's coastal wetlands, inhibiting businesses there from doing much besides aquaculture. The mangrove forests are a haven for many species and provide unique coastal protection from environmental disasters of both the natural and man-made varieties.

THE BEAUTIFUL BADJAO

Ask any tricycle driver (lingo for a bicycle or motorbike with a sidecar), or indeed any local, and he or she will happily point you in the right direction. The Badjao Seafront Restaurant owners cut a half-mile-long wooden walkway into the jungle from the mainland side, and the walkway leads to a long, narrow teak deck. You realize about halfway down that you are walking along a wooden pathway set on stilts, and beneath you are the swampy waters off the Sulu Sea. At the end of this walkway, sitting like a glowing fireplace on a cold winter's day, is a gorgeous teak and mahogany restaurant, built on top of a floating raft, poking out into the bay.

Our local tourism department contacts and I sit down at Badjao and soak up the 270-degree view of the bay, dotted with small sampans, little fishing and shrimping boats, gliding along one of the pristine inner bays of the Sulu Sea, framed by a horizon of mountains. The menu reads like a greatest-hits list of the best of Philippines seafood cuisine. I was blown away when I saw fresh whelks sautéed in coconut milk with shredded banana flowers making its way to another table, and I almost fainted with happiness when I peeked at the menu and saw it priced at three dollars a pop.

I took on the task of paring lunch down to seven or eight dishes. Luckily, everyone was into sharing. Our server offered up a mango-and-banana shake to tide us over. This was no ordinary shake. The Badjao Seafront Restaurant plucks the juiciest mangoes straight off the trees, adds bananas from the huge four-and-a-half-foot-tall bunch leaning on the bar, purees the fruit with a bit of ice and a splash of water, and sticks a straw in the result. I should tell you that the number-one agricultural force in Palawan are the banana farms—which produce bananas of such sweet and primal excellence that you won't tire of them showing up at every meal. Roadside stands sell banana-Q, a local treat made by rolling fresh, ripe bananas on sticks in a bowl of crushed brown sugar and deep-frying them. It's like a candy apple mated with bananas

Foster, just absent the snooty waiter and the rolling table-side cart.

As we awaited the arrival of our food, I wandered around the side of the restaurant, hoping to catch a glimpse of the fishermen navigating their miniature flat-bottom boats. I looked on as they fished about a mile out from the restaurant, collecting shrimp and snapper from their little clusters of nets. It was a physical endeavor—pushing and pulling themselves around the bay, tossing nets, reeling them in, then poling or paddling back over to the restaurant, where they would disappear from view. I walked to the edge of the deck, only to discover that they were hoisting baskets of fresh fish, shrimp, and crabs directly from the bay to the kitchen window, where the contents would be dispatched and, within minutes, arrive at our table.

OUR MENU

I'd pinned myself down to the grilled shrimp, the monstrously large sautéed crayfish, and snails with the coconut milk and banana flower—a dish that I had always wanted to try but hadn't had the opportunity. The flower is the sturdy purple cone-shaped flower that grows from the bottom of the master cluster of bananas. The banana flower is available anywhere bananas grow, and every time I have seen it, since tasting it for the first time in Palawan, I have asked if it's used in the local food. From Puerto Rico to Nicaragua, Okinawa to Samoa: it's an emphatic no. Filipinos, on the other hand, are addicted to cooking with it. The flower is sliced paper thin on a mandoline or, if the chef has excellent knife skills, cut by hand into little shreds; then it is sautéed with coconut milk. The flowers pair perfectly with something saline and gamy, like snails.

We dined on teeny grilled fish, served with Philippine soy sauce and a squeeze of kalamansi—a gumball-size citrus fruit that's a cross between a lime and a tangerine. Kalamansi is to Palawan what salt and pepper is to America: readily available and dispensed on everything. The grill was fired by fresh coconut husks, which impart a superb light smokiness to the food. The grilled shrimp and mackerel actually melt in your mouth. Seafood lumpia were rolled and fried to order, the whelks with banana flower had a strong injection of lime before they left the kitchen, and no one at the table could resist inhaling the food as it came in waves on groaning platters from the kitchen. With all the commotion over the ceaseless flow of dish after amazing dish (not to mention the fact that I was overeating to begin with), I'd completely forgotten about the final item, which had yet to emerge from the kitchen. I'd seen tuna collar on the menu and thought, Gee, what a nice little treat. I'll have some tuna collar.

Even casual fans of Japanese food are used to the minuscule *hamachi* (young yellowtail tuna) collars sold in just about every Japanese restaurant. Roughly the size of a small envelope and about an inch thick, those collars are lightly salted to dry out some of the moisture, then broiled and served with grated daikon radish, a squirt of lemon juice, and soy sauce. The collar bone is laden with fatty, rich bits of flesh, and it's worth every minute of the canoodling it takes to extract the tasty morsels. That's half the fun, like a treasure hunt, and it's addictive, so I was looking forward to trying Badjao's version despite my straining waistline.

THE FINAL "ILLEGAL" DISH

We'd finished up most of lunch when I realized, Hmm . . . no tuna collar. Assuming they'd simply forgotten, I asked our server where my tuna collar was and I was calmly informed that it was still cooking.

As I'm discussing the situation with our server, out comes the tuna collar, spilling over the edges of a twenty-four-inch-long platter. Here is Badjao's version of this culinary gem: a seven- or eight-pound Flintstone-size roast of bone and meat from a gigantic yellowfin or bluefin tuna. This fish had to weigh several hundred pounds when it landed in the boat. Brushed with sweet rice wine and soy sauce, served with fresh chilies and those little kalamansi, this collar was quite the indulgent dish.

Foodies obsess about illegal foods like ortolans of Western Europe—about devouring whole roasted teensy birdies drowned in Armagnac while covering one's head with a napkin to assuage the guilt. People wax poetic about attending foie gras orgies in New York's underground restaurants. Sure, you can have all that stuff, but the rarest of rare food experiences is the opportunity to eat something unique, in the main because the ingredients aren't available in any other spot in the world. An open source of giant fish, where chefs have inexpensive access to pristine precious ingredients, exists in very few places in the world. Consider this: at Tokyo's

Tsukiji Market, just the collar alone would cost thousands of dollars, and here I was, for the equivalent of a few dollars, chomping away at this giant, charred, fatty piece of tuna goodness. I didn't have to force myself to eat the whole thing; I had a little help from my traveling mates.

Going to the last stop on the subway in the Philippines afforded me the opportunity to dine in an environment where I wasn't competing with too many people, finding ingredients in their own *terroir*, so to speak (with a neutral carbon footprint, no less!), and without paying through the nose. Eat the same dish halfway around the world from there and not only will it be expensive and somewhat ginned up, but the flavor will be compromised, the experience diluted to the point that it is almost not worth having. If something is worth eating, it's worth eating well.

Muddy Waters: Ugandan Lungfishing Can Be Messy

"Lungfish" is the common name for a primitive, freshwater, air-breathing fish that resides exclusively in tropical areas of Australia, Africa, and South America. Only six species of lungfish survive today, but fossil records tell us that lungfish were much more widespread and in more plentifully differentiated species in the distant past. Scientists agree that **lungfish** are closely related to the ancestors of the earliest vertebrates that adapted to live on land, which is very important, because lungfish are extremely unusual animals.

> The three families of lungfish are Lepidosirenidae (South American lungfish), Protopteridae (African lungfish), and Ceratodidae (Australian lungfish).

THE FISHY FACTS

The name itself refers to the specialized lung that serves as the creature's main organ for breathing. This lung allows the fish to gulp air as an adaptation to low-oxygen water environments, such as swamps or bodies of water that frequently dry up.

Most fish use their gills to pull the oxygen out of the water. Lungfish also have gills, but theirs are relatively small compared to those of their fellow denizens of the deep. Young African lungfish have true external gills, which degenerate with age. The single lung on most species of lungfish is more like a modified swim bladder, the air-filled organ that almost all fish use to help them float at a particular depth, saving energy while swimming around the ocean, but in lungfish the modified swim bladder can also absorb oxygen. Freaky!

When kicking back and chilling out, lungfish excrete carbon dioxide through their gills or skin, just like most other fish, but most other fish get oxygen only through their gills. The special lung of the lungfish also removes carbon dioxide waste when the lungfish is very active, an anomaly in the underwater world. African lungfish actually rise to the surface to breathe and can "drown" without access to air.

Lungfish have elongated **bodies** with a double set of fleshy limbs that resemble cylindrical fins. Their oddly shaped, fanlike **teeth,** which act like an under-the-counter

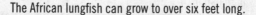
The African lungfish can grow to over six feet long.

Lungfish are predators and will eat nearly anything. Their diet consists mainly of fish, crayfish, and crabs. They're fearless and will attack almost anything that moves, including human hands.

trash compactor, are ideally suited to their diet of fish, insects, mollusks, worms, crustaceans, and plants. These fish are very territorial and extremely aggressive. They build nests where the male protects the eggs laid by the female until they hatch.

African lungfish estivate, meaning they can become dormant, hibernating during dry periods or droughts for a few months if need be. If necessary, they can sleep for years at a time—that's years . . . plural! They burrow into the mud and secrete a covering of mucus around themselves. The mucus hardens into a cocoon, but a small, closable breathing hole is left in the mummylike covering. The fish reduce their metabolism to a bare whisper and simply shut down. The protective cocoon softens when it gets wet—say, at the end of the dry season—and the fish can reemerge and live in the water again.

Lungfish, like their cousin the coelacanth, are commonly thought of as living fossils—a reference to the fact that these animals have essentially remained physically unchanged for hundreds of millions of years.

Oh yeah, and one more thing: when lungfish are in that cocoon and they get hungry, they consume their own body tissues . . . and once they come out of it, they grow back to their original size.

But let's start from the beginning. The moment Travel Channel picked up *Bizarre Foods*, I wanted to live for a time with an African tribe. It seemed to me to be the ultimate family of *Bizarre Foods* experiences: Getting in with real indigenous people, many of whom live the same way their ancestors did thousands of years ago, would allow me the best opportunities to experience food and share cultures. And that's exactly what we found in Uganda.

Uganda is located in East Africa, and it is landlocked by Kenya, Tanzania, Rwanda, Zaire, and Sudan. Much like its neighbors', Uganda's past has been turbulent at times. Despite the fact that Uganda achieved independence from Britain in 1962, the establishment of a working political community has been a Herculean task, due to the ethnic diversity of the population.

You're probably wondering if this is a safe place to be traveling to begin with. I had plenty of those thoughts myself, and it seemed anytime I researched this trip, I stumbled upon words like "insurgent activity," "armed banditry," and "roadside ambushes." We were staying in the city of Kampala, located on the northern edge of Africa's largest body of water, **Lake Victoria,** for the first few days and last night of our stay, but for the greater part of our trip we lived in an isolated village well outside the city. I always felt very safe in Uganda, but that's a relative term. Flying in to Entebbe International Airport, you can see the decades-old hull of the famous Air France jet hijacked in 1976, now left as a "training

---

Lake Victoria is the main reservoir of the Nile River and is the largest lake in Africa. Lake Victoria occupies an area of approximately 26,800 square miles and is the second-largest freshwater lake in the world, after Lake Superior in North America.

tool" on the runway where it finally came to rest. Not the most charming of welcome mats. Armed guards, hired to keep us safe, watched over us in Lwanika. Frankly, I wondered how one old guy with a rusty AK-47 would fare against a jeep- or truckload of rebels intending to do us harm or steal our equipment. I bet my producer a hundred bucks that the rifle couldn't fire if he pulled the trigger a dozen times, which was a bet he wouldn't take.

VISITING THE VILLAGERS

We headed out by Range Rover to Lwanika, where we would stay with the Embegge tribe for four days. We started off on a main, paved highway heading out from the city of Kampala, snagged up for a good half hour in the early-morning traffic of the congested city. Eventually, that road morphs into a simple paved road, then to a dirt road, and finally you're actually going all-terrain, driving over rutted grass byways to get to the heart of the village. In and around the village itself, we encountered a system of primitive dirt roads that connect the isolated villages of the region to each other. Villagers from one cluster of simple mud and straw homes would walk or bike from one to another to visit family or friends, or to help with work.

While it's extremely rare for most **villagers** to venture into the big city, modern civilization has touched their lives

 Native Africans have been found to dig up lungfish, burrow and all, and store them for later use when they want fresh fish to eat. Now, that's a serious doggie bag!

just enough that they have the occasional need to go into another village or a bigger town. The most traveled members of the tribes always seemed to be those involved with dance or music, and most of these villagers spent a lot of time traveling throughout eastern Africa performing in regional festivals and contests.

This explains why the Embegge in Lwanika greeted us with an impressive amount of fanfare. All the women turned out, dancing and singing us into the main town square—just a dirt area surrounded by a cluster of four or five homes. It seemed everyone was curious about the arrival of these *"bazungu"* and their cameras. **Muzungu** basically means

 The term for white Westerners is *muzungu* (plural *bazungu*). Caucasian visitors should get used to hearing it shouted out by children in every corner of the country. It is not a derogatory term, so smile and wave.

"whitey" in Ugandan culture, but it never felt derogatory—people use it more as a term of endearment mixed with a healthy dose of good humor. In fact, this nickname put me at ease and made me feel so welcome that I went so far as to join the village's all-female cooking co-op for an adventurous lesson in cooking matooke—a common dish made from boiled and mashed green bananas. To the Embegge, this was probably the most bizarre thing they'd ever seen from any man, as the responsibility of preparing food—except for lungfish—belongs solely to **females.** In fact, once a male hits age twelve, he isn't expected to even sit in the kitchen. Taking an active role in the people's everyday lives, instead of simply staring and gawking from the safety of my Land Rover

> In Uganda, females do not eat the lungfish because they consider it a "sister fish." Men assume the task of preparing (and eating) the lungfish.

as most visitors do, afforded me a singular experience that meant we bonded in a way that would have been impossible had I only hung out for a few hours a day, then bussed back to a cushy hotel room somewhere.

A DAY IN THE LIFE

Life for the Embegge is very rustic compared to life in the city of **Kampala.** For the most part, they do not wear Western clothes in the American sense. Women wear a traditional native shift, the same sacklike dress they've been wearing for years. Men wear pants and T-shirts in the village, or just shorts and flip-flops. Young men in Lwanika dress like beach bums in Hawaii. But because national charitable organizations in the States organize fund-raising drives on a grass-roots level, you will often see whole families or villages decked out in prom shirts from 1997 in Cleveland, or see three boys walking together across a jungle field all wearing "Kimmelman Bar Mitzvah 2006, WE LOVE YOU KENNY!" tees. The families live in small, circular mud and straw huts, which they share with their goats, cows, or other animals, depending on which predators live in the jungles nearby.

> Intertribal marriage is still rare in Uganda, and although many Kampala residents have been born and bred in the city, they still define themselves by their tribal roots.

Some families are situated in homes made of brick with penned enclosures for their animals. This is becoming more and more the norm. They cook over small fires, and they farm and hunt off the surrounding land, sharing what they can with their community. It's the pinnacle of sustainable living, except that buzzword doesn't exist here. It's just the only way of life they know.

The Embegge people were gracious, kind, and generous hosts, more welcoming than I could ever have imagined. However, I'd be lying if I said the few days I spent with them weren't one of the most physically, mentally, and emotionally stressful experiences of my life. You're constantly fighting the oppressive dampness and moisture, the heat, the hunger, the overwhelming stench of rotting plant matter, and the constant threat of disease. It's how I'd imagine August in the Everglades, except with more animals that can eat you and insects that can kill you, plus the fact that the nearest person who can understand you is thousands of miles away.

From dusk until dawn, all *bazungu* must cover themselves from head to toe in clothing that has been treated with permethrin, a powerful insecticide that you must soak your clothing in, and wear heavy-duty DEET repellant. Despite the fact that you've essentially bathed in these chemicals, the biting flies, some literally the size of cigar butts, continue to seek whatever purchase on you they can. At night, from the safety of our fire and wrapped tighter than Tutankhamen in fine cheesecloth, we could see the mosquitoes flying in cloud-like waves around our heads.

I was quickly forced to face my fears on day two as I accompanied some of the tribesmen on a lungfish hunt. To be perfectly honest, I was really nervous about going lungfishing from the first days of preproduction because of the horrific swamps in which they live. I was petrified of disappearing in a mud suck-hole or being devoured by snakes.

CATCHING MY FIRST LUNGFISH

Early that morning, eight of us marched from our tents through the jungle to the swampy rice paddies where the tribe farmed their grain. There were dozens of paddies, each a couple of acres in size, all bordered by mud berms made of swamp detritus. Reeds, branches, and grasses are cut by hand and piled like dikes between the ponds to regulate the flow. These organic items decompose very rapidly, creating a mud topped by spongy, grassy compost, which serves as pathways between ponds after years of being cut and piled and shaped. The waters here are filled with poisonous snakes—several of the most deadly varieties in the world, in fact—as well as some of the most infamous disease-carrying insects. The mud berms were so brutish to walk on, they actually sucked my Keens right off my feet. I went barefoot for most of the day after that, encouraged by local pals who reminded me that the only thing in the water was mud and plant life. A lot could happen to me out there, but stubbed toes and cut feet were essentially physical impossibilities. I had envisioned my body helplessly succumbing to the mud after accidentally stepping in a sinkhole, however, so I insisted on tying a rope around my waist—just in case.

Catching a lungfish is nothing like any sort of fishing I've ever done. First, you take a giant stick outfitted with four or five metal barbs, which are typically just pieces of stiff wire lashed to the end of the poles. It resembles a supersize fondue fork, maybe six feet long. Next, you jab the pole into these grassy, muddy walls, trying to find hollow spots where the fish nest. Occasionally, you'll spot a fish as it surfaces, breaking the thick brown water for a breath of fresh air.

The lungfish we found were about four feet long, weighed twenty-five to forty pounds, and had ferociously large teeth sprouting from their powerful jaws. They are extremely ugly and angry animals, and, as it turns out, they don't like to have their nests poked by *bazungu*. They like it even less when, upon finding their nest, you start hacking away at the mud walls with a machete. Here's the best part: Once these crazed, prehistoric creatures start to slither in, around, or out of their nest, you must blindly reach down into the mud and muck and retrieve them by hand. And considering their giant, sharp teeth, you better hope you find them before they find you. As you're trying to get your hands on the fish, your fishing mates attempt to jab the fondue forks into the fish to immobilize them. Trust plays an important role in lungfishing.

All the lungfish that we caught were found by hand, then speared once they were found. Holding on to a wiggling, thirty-odd-pound, ferocious half-fish, half-lizard animal, all while standing chest deep in filthy stagnant water in the middle of the Ugandan jungle surrounded by biting flies, leeches, ticks, snakes, and God knows what else, was one of the more intimidating experiences of my life. I couldn't have been happier that catching them actually happened a lot faster than I'd anticipated. Within an hour, we had five or six lungfish sprinkled throughout our eight-man fishing party. Surprisingly, I'd landed one on my second try. The guides were cheering and screaming *"Muzungu! Muzungu!"* the entire time. Apparently, they had never seen a white person even try to catch lungfish, let alone actually score one. I am proud of many achievements in my life, but having dubbed myself the first muzungu lungfisherman in Lwanika is one of my all-time faves.

COOKING WITH NATURE

By this time in the morning, it had to be ninety-five degrees, with 80 percent humidity. We were all a dirty, muddy, sweaty mess, and I was just so thankful that the ordeal of collecting food was over. We carried the fish, impaled on our spears, over our shoulders and back to camp. Interestingly, lungfish is one of the few foods the women will not prepare, and therefore the men take a turn in the kitchen. Whereas in larger African cities a salt and sun-dried method is commonly used in preparing the fish, the tribesmen usually hot-smoke them. This fancy-food term brings to mind images of these wonderful, touristy salmon shops in the Pacific Northwest, which couldn't be further from reality.

The Embegge build a huge fire of brushwood, then place the fish fillets on a cooking grate, drying and charring them in the fire's smoke. Once the process is completed, you end up with an overcooked, rock-hard, brown and blackened slab of fish. In that state, it continues to dry out and can later be rehydrated in boiling water and braised in a stew with g-nuts, which are what we would call peanuts here at home. Peanuts are incorporated into a lot of Ugandan and East African cuisine, commonly mixed into a paste with sesame seeds and used as a condiment for meat, or crushed and served sautéed with greens, steamed with beans and rice, or boiled in a soup that's used to rehydrate the lungfish, which is exactly what we did.

This was one-pot cooking in its purest form. The fish reminded me of carp, an oversize whitefish I've eaten plenty of in my time: kind of fatty, a bit fibrous, but definitely mild. This ferocious, prehistoric animal was more benign on the palate than I ever imagined. In fact, I've discovered that most of the time, the more ferocious and horrific-looking something is in real life, the more mild the flavor and the duller the eating experience.

As we prepared our meal, I couldn't help but think about how many times this scene is repeated over and over again in every African village. Whether the villagers are lungfishing or collecting wild vegetables, seeking out ingredients is such hard work that they collect the bare minimum of food, gathering only what is needed that day. They really don't have a place to store food effectively before it starts to go bad, bananas and grains being the two large exceptions. We caught five or six lungfish, well over the normal daily quota, because the entire village was turning out that night for the big dinner celebration.

In addition to the lungfish, the Embegge killed a goat for stewing, something typically reserved for special occasions. That night we ate the fish, the goat, roast squirrel, flying ants, crickets, millet porridge, rice and beans, g-nuts, matooke, yucca, cassava, and sweet potatoes and other root vegetables that are commonly served in tribal Uganda. You see more unseasoned, nasty root vegetables in tribal East Africa than anywhere else in the world. I'd be just fine if I never saw another steamed potato—or steamed banana—again after my three-week visit there.

Not a day goes by that I don't think of the Embegge. The journey was difficult, the stress was insane, and the unknown was all around you every second of every day, but the simple fact of the matter was that for four days I never once thought of a bill I had to pay or a call I had to make.

Saving Huatulco:
Free Diving for Octopus

It might not seem like it at first glance, but Mexico is one of the world's most diverse countries, ethnically, geographically, politically, and culturally. Every time I visit, I marvel at the abundance of things to do and how amazingly different one day can be from another. Americans love heading to Cabo, Mazatlán, or Cozumel, but my favorite destination has to be the country's southernmost state, **Oaxaca**. I'm sure you've heard of Acapulco, the region's most bustling beach town, but beyond that, Oaxaca offers the best of everything: gorgeous sand beaches, a phenomenally complex and varied

> How do you say the *x* in *Oaxaca*? The *x* in Spanish is pronounced like an *h*. Therefore, *Oaxaca* sounds like "wah-HAH-kah."

food scene, and (in most towns) that easygoing vibe that nobody I know can ever seem to get enough of.

The Pacific coast of the state of Oaxaca is lined from top to bottom with fishing villages, both large and small, some thriving, some dying, and some struggling to survive the onslaught of the developers' bulldozers. Take the city of Huatulco, which seemed to spring up almost overnight, but really has grown over the past three or four decades from a lonely little beach, with some fun rock outcroppings surrounding a nice deep-water harbor, into a numbingly throbbing hotel zone. Back in the day, this little beach town was wallowing in huge puddles of financial success because of the fishing. The sheer abundance of seafood that is available here is staggering: Mollusks, abalone, conch and clams, urchins, squid, fin fish, lobsters—you can find all manner of crustaceans in the cool, deep waters off Huatulco. These days, tourism drives the economy. Projections are that the once-tiny fishing town will support some twenty thousand hotel rooms by 2020. In 2008, nearly 300,000 visitors traveled to Huatulco. Within twenty years, that number is expected to swell to 2 million.

I spent some time in Huatulco a few years back, staying overnight in one of those all-inclusive resorts on the beachfront. I've said it before and I'll say it again: The best experiences you will ever have as a traveler require getting off your bottom and spending quality time with real people in real towns, cities, and villages. I prefer to do it by experiencing food and sharing culture.

While I love the Pacific shellfish, Huatulco is actually best known for a different sort of sea creature. The area surrounding the town's hotel zone, technically called Las Bahías de Huatulco, is made up of about nine bays that stretch for twenty miles along southern Mexico's Pacific shore. Much of the coastline is extremely rocky, with good currents and clean waters, and thus provides the perfect breeding grounds for **octopus.** I love hunting and gathering food, so naturally I wanted to fish for octopus the old-fashioned way.

 Octopuses are rarely kept in captivity, in part because of their well-known problem-solving skills and high intelligence, which has been compared to that of the average house cat. They've been known to escape tanks and aquariums with great ease.

OCTOPUS DIVING WITH FRANCISCO

Enter Francisco Rios Ramirez, an octopus diver with thirty years' experience under his belt. Francisco has a trim waistline, maybe thirty-four inches, but the guy weighs more than I do. He's solid muscle, with a huge chest and the widest shoulders I have seen on anyone his size. If I hadn't known better, I would have pegged him as an NFL linebacker, albeit a very short one. My crew and I met up with him at the docks in the sleepy port of Santa Cruz. We shared a coffee and a roll, got our gear together, and, under a cloudless sky, boarded his little boat, a skiff with an ancient outboard motor, and headed out toward our first stop, Tagolunda

Bay—the name, incidentally, means "beautiful woman" in Zapotec, one of the area's indigenous languages.

Francisco dives into the bays in the area nearly every day of the week, bringing in anywhere from twenty to forty octopuses per trip, each of which weighs roughly two **pounds.** His method is ancient and bare-bones, to say the least. Armed with only a thin, yard-long metal stick with a hook attached to the end of it, and wearing only a tight, faded Speedo, some cracked flippers, and an ancient diving mask, he flips over the gunwale and out of the boat. I follow him. He starts out by diving twenty feet under the water and hovering there for a minute or two. At this point, he's not even looking for octopus, just checking out the visibility and current, but all the while he's expanding his lungs' capacity to hold oxygen. By the time he finds a good spot to look for octopus, he's able to hold his breath for four or five minutes, which seems like an eternity when you're sitting in the boat or floating nearby hoping your diving buddy—and only means of transport back to shore—isn't dead.

> The second-largest type of octopus in the world is the North Pacific octopus, which can grow to thirty feet and weigh up to one hundred pounds. The smallest species is the California octopus, which maxes out at about an inch.

Francisco started me out on a few of the tamer dives, but after a few short lessons, we were off in search of our catch together. I should remind you at this point that I am five feet ten inches tall, weigh 240 pounds, and exercise as often as I can, which is about once a month. My idea of fun water sports is not heading ten miles from the nearest dock and free diving in deep water with a swift current in the middle of the Pacific Ocean. But sitting with Francisco, prodded by his immensely toothy grin and halting guarantees of my safety, with my kitchen Spanish as our only means of communication, gave me all the confidence I needed. Besides, if we catch octopus, we eat octopus, right?

TAKING IN OUR SURROUNDINGS

The water in Tagolunda Bay, especially at the two outermost points of the bay, was some of the cleanest, most pristine ocean that I've ever spent time in. The seabed here is composed entirely of rocks and boulders, which means that there is no sand to be stirred up and cloud the water. These conditions are what Francisco looks for in a good octopus bed. You could see hundreds of feet in every direction. The water was teeming with bait and sport fish. The morning sun afforded us some incredible light as it entered the water. It was just absolutely breathtaking.

I wish I could have enjoyed the setting as much as I would have liked while I was in the water itself. Even though I was with a pro, my nervousness wouldn't subside. I was in water up to forty feet deep and fighting a ferocious current. In this part of the Pacific, you need to be careful not to get too close to shore or the rolling surf will smash you against the rocks. The entire time I was diving, I struggled to stay at least twenty-five feet off the shore, simply holding my position so I wouldn't get distracted and, subsequently, pulverized.

Of course, octopuses aren't always such easy picking. When they aren't feeding, they tend to squeeze their **invertebrate bodies** into the rocky nooks and crannies. Francisco poked around the large, round boulders that made up the underwater terrain, trying to coax the little cephalopods into the open. If he can't grab them with his hand, he'll hook them and place them in his free hand. Oddly enough, the octopus inadvertently aids this part of the process by clinging to your hand with its suction-cup-covered **tentacles.** Once back floating alongside the boat, Francisco demonstrated how to hold the octopus by putting your finger in and around the area of its **mouth,** which sits on the underside of the head, and sort of squeezing and holding him there. Don't put your fingers directly in its mouth. Octopuses have sturdy beaks, and trust me, you don't want to get nipped by an octopus beak.

~The majority of octopuses have almost entirely soft bodies with no internal skeleton. That means no protective outer shell or internal bones. This enables them to squeeze through narrow crevices—helpful when trying to outrun predators.

~Octopuses have an excellent sense of touch. Their tentacles are equipped with suction cups that not only help them grip but also allow them to taste whatever they're touching.

~The only hard part on an octopus's body is the beak, which resembles a parrot's.

Within a few hours, we'd filled our boat with all the octopus we had come for, but Francisco wanted to make a few more stops on the way back to Santa Cruz and the dock. On our return trip, we went through the majestic Chahue Bay.

The views here were nothing short of stunning: limestone cliffs dramatically plunging into the water, giant boulders with waves slapping over them. We dropped anchor and dove back into the water to scare up a few more octopuses and take advantage of a little more underwater sightseeing before we headed back to a small town called La Crucecita. This is a charming seafront village that boasts some of the best seafood restaurants in southern Mexico, including El Grillo Marinero, which Francisco and his wife of twenty-six years, Pola, own.

> While many octopuses are good eating, some species are very poisonous. Rule of thumb: The smaller the octopus, the more poisonous it is. The most deadly species is the blue-ringed octopus. Found mainly in Pacific Ocean tide pools off the coasts of Australia and Japan, this small speckled creature produces venom strong enough to kill a human.

While the shrimp and local red snapper are delicious, the *especialidad de la casa* is *pulpo*, or octopus. After we dropped our catch in the kitchen, Francisco went to get cleaned up. I stayed behind in the kitchen with Pola, who is known as one of the region's best seafood chefs. Cooking octopus is a tough job, but Pola works efficiently and quickly, meticulously cleaning each octopus, discarding the head and viscera, preserving the ink sac for later use. Next, she butchers the octopuses and tenderizes the tentacles by pounding them by hand against a large stone perched next to the sink.

Lucky for me, all the octopuses here are small, and Pola made short work of kicking out several different versions of the house specialty, each one tasting more delicious and complex than the last. Francisco returned to the dining room and we sat down to eat. Pola started us off with octopus and shrimp cocktail, made up of steamed diced octopus and poached shrimp, cooled and sauced with onions, garlic, lime juice, cilantro, and fresh tomatoes, and served in a tall sundae glass with spoons and fresh tortilla chips. Think cold poached seafood that melts in your mouth bathed in the best gazpacho you can imagine. As we inhaled that dish, the octopus platters came rolling out of the kitchen one at a time.

POLA'S MENU

Next was Creole-style Mexican octopus, sautéed with some garlic and onions, fresh tomatoes and peppers, and finished with a little bit of wine, braised all together for fifteen or twenty minutes and served in its own reduced pan sauce with some rice and soft corn tortillas.

The second dish was fresh octopus cooked in wine with garlic and a healthy dose of the octopus ink. I adored this octopus version of a squid dish I first ate with my dad forty years ago when we traveled to Venice. The rich, thick black sauce that coats the octopus is slightly citrusy, and redolent in the most profound way of the dark, briny ocean. There is an earthy and deeply nutty taste that squid and octopus have, and cooking the animal in its own ink makes the perfect combination, not only allowing the whole animal to be used at once but also providing a beautiful flavor contrast thanks to the slightly lemony edge this particular ink offers.

But the dish that absolutely blew my mind was the garlic-and-salt-glazed pulpo al ajillo, which is a very traditional

Oaxacan treatment and a centerpiece of southern Mexico's grandmother cuisine. It's a dish rarely found in restaurants. Pola takes ten cloves of garlic and about a teaspoon of sea salt and pounds these into a fine paste in her mortar, rolling the pestle around the interior of the vessel with quick, precise strokes. There is not a bit of garlic that's larger than a grain of sand left in her mortar. Pola turns a burner on the stove to a very low setting and gets the pan hot. Keeping the burner on low, she puts a little bit of olive oil in the pan and begins to sauté the garlic-and-salt paste until it's cooked through, custardy yellow and sweet to the taste, without that scorching acrid quality to it. She then adds the octopus, cut into pieces, and cooks it for a few moments, then adds a splash of wine, covers the pan, and cooks it for about twenty minutes more, or until the octopus is tender. She takes the lid off and she lets the sauce and liquid cook down until it has evaporated entirely around the octopus, leaving all the flavor of that winey sauce concentrated inside this dish. All that is left other than the octopus is the garlic and olive oil; the liquids have done their job. She cranks up the heat for the last fifty seconds, basically caramelizing the garlic in the oil-coated seafood, where it clings to the octopus like a supersweet garlic candy coating. Now the octopus itself melts in your mouth with a sweet, earthy flavor that drove me nuts.

Some people are crazy about garlic; I'm not one of them. But this garlicky paste of goodness made for one of the best dishes I have ever eaten in my entire life, a simple technique-driven dish that I have made over and over again back home, using everything from shrimp to chicken. It's easy.

WHEN TOURISM TAKES OVER

Hand-fishing for octopus on a sunny day in the Pacific is deceptively intoxicating, but long afterward I was stuck thinking about the future of fishermen like Francisco. His tiny town of La Crucecita and the once-sleepy port of Santa Cruz, where there was a vibrant fishing industry just a generation ago, is now home to parasailing, scuba-diving, and sea-kayaking companies. The town's native culture is in desperate trouble due to tourism companies that can drop serious cash for the dockside real estate. They're squeezing out people like Francisco, whose family is one of the original five that founded the towns back in the day when there was only fishing.

Unfortunately, tourism is not the only industry that has discovered this beautiful place. Giant fishing trawlers scoop up bycatch by the tens of thousands, meaning that in addition to the fish they're intending to catch, they also bring in piles of unwanted fish and critters (like turtles, sharks, and dolphins). These untargeted catches often die, which makes sustaining native fish populations next to impossible. I love seafood more than anyone, but this method of fishing is irresponsible—it will likely result not only in the extinction of certain species, but in the certain deterioration of our oceans.

ALTERNATIVE EATING

Promoting artisan fishing would certainly help this community, as well as its volatile ecosystem. Francisco's operation, old-school as it may be, is a model for how we can make it work. Take the animals by hand, catch only what you need, and let the fishery self-regulate. Once trawlers are sent packing, the octopus population will rebound quickly, due to the species' ability to reproduce in a short amount of time.

Of course, getting people to care about an alternative protein, like octopus, is a hurdle in and of itself. While octopus is wildly popular in most other parts of the world, Americans perceive shrimp, black cod, tuna, and salmon as the sea fare with the most sex appeal and most table-friendly attributes. However, octopus (and the small whole fishes that the rest of the world eats regularly) should be on everyone's radar and dining room table. These are some of the best-flavored kinds of sea fare, high in protein, low in calories, usually inexpensive, and fairly easy to prepare. Eating alternative proteins is the only way to ease the pressure on center-of-the-plate commodity foods like chicken, pork, and beef. Octopus is not a novelty item. It represents our salvation, and that was one of the reasons I wanted to go diving with Francisco in the first place.

Death Match: Can a Matador Save Madrid's Historic Tabernas?

A restaurant has a life span much like a dog's. If it lasts seven or eight years, it has lived a healthy and decent life. If it makes it to ten or twelve, and can put a little money back into the investors' pockets after paying off its opening and carrying costs, it's had a really good life. But if a restaurant is a couple of hundred years old, passed down from generation to generation, and manages to continue serving up one of the best versions of its country's national dish, which once fueled the most macho elements of the local culture—well, a restaurant of that caliber is more than just a precious family heirloom, it's a national treasure.

MADRID: A CITY OF ABUNDANT CUISINE

Madrid has truly earned its chops as one of the world's great eating cities, and simply walking down its winding cobblestone streets really got my taste buds going. Madrid's food scene is made up of two very distinct culinary styles: traditional Spanish cuisine and extremely modern.

TRADITION: TAPAS

It is often joked that Madrid's restaurants outnumber the local populace by about three to one, and Spaniards take advantage of that abundance every few hours. They not only eat—they enjoy food. And there is a big difference between mechanical and mindful eating. Business or social conversation is an excuse for snacking, and Spaniards have no issue with partaking of a leisurely lunch or eating well into the night, usually not even starting dinner until ten p.m. Remember, Spain is the culture that gave us **tapas** in the first place.

> The Spanish are night owls, and dinner rarely starts before ten p.m. Of course, the time span between lunch and dinner is great, so Spaniards fill their tummies with tapas, or small plates of food meant to be shared. The postwork crowd fills tapas bars for snacks, often visiting a few in one evening.

There are a few ideas as to how this small-plate style of eating came to be. Some people will tell you it comes from farmworkers needing small bits of food to hold them over until the day's main meal was served. Others claim a Spanish king came up with the concept. By law, every drink needed to be served with a bit of food to soak up the alcohol in order to sober up the wine-guzzling workforce. In any case, it's a brilliant idea that still shapes the local and global food scene. In Spain, tapas just sprouted organically. It's a grazing culture: You eat a wonderful breakfast and spend an hour or two enjoying a leisurely lunch. Midafternoon, you might stop at a ham shop before heading home after the day's work. From seven p.m. until ten, you eat tapas and drink with your friends.

THE MUSEUM OF HAM

My tapas crawl that evening ended at Museo del Jamón, one of a small chain of ham restaurants that are really cathedrals of worship for eaters like myself. The name translates roughly as "museum of ham." But the idea that great cured meats are under glass and safely away from overeager mouths, accessed only by an audio tour headset, is far from the case. Stroll into the store and all around you are belly-button-high marble counters behind which are more types of cured sausages, cured meats, meat salads, and traditional salume-style fare than you've ever seen in your life, hundreds and hundreds of varieties. Of course, they offer the all-star **Ibérico** dried and cured hams as well as Serrano hams, Spain's version of prosciutto. Their Bellota ham was arguably the finest cured

 Iberian ham, or *jamón ibérico,* is one of the most prized meats in the world. The black Iberian pig lives primarily in the south and southwest parts of Spain. The pigs mostly chow down on barley, maize, herbs, roots, and acorns. In the weeks prior to slaughter, the pigs eat only acorns.

ham I had ever eaten; you could taste the wild-pig goodness, the acorn and hazelnut diet, the delicate **salting** and air drying, and the thin yellow fat streaked through the meat and edging each slice tasted almost as divinely musty as the season's first truffle. I know this sounds weird, but I love to wash down a meal at Museo del Jamón with a tall glass of freshly squeezed orange juice. To me, it's the perfect combination—like chocolate chip cookies and milk.

After slaughter, the pigs are salted and left to dry for two weeks. They're then rinsed and left to dry for another four to six weeks. While the hams are often cured for a year, some producers will age their hams for up to three.

Even if the only Spanish phrase you know is *"¿Dónde está el baño?"* you can still navigate a tapas menu with this handy guide.

Aceitunas: Olives.

Albóndigas: Meatballs.

Bacalao: Dried salted codfish, served very thinly sliced and usually with bread and tomatoes.

Boquerones: White anchovies served in vinegar or deep-fried.

Calamares: Squid, cut in rings, dipped in batter, and deep-fried.

Chopitos: Tiny cuttlefish, battered and deep-fried. Also known as puntillitas.

Chorizo a la sidra: Chorizo sausage slowly cooked in cider.

Croquetas: Small croquettes, a common sight on bar counters and in homes across Spain, served as a tapa, a light lunch, or a dinner along with a salad.

Empanadas: Large or small turnovers filled with meats and vegetables.

Jamón ibérico: A prized Spanish cured ham known for its smooth texture and rich, savory taste

Manchego: A cheese made in the La Mancha region of Spain from sheep's milk, aged anywhere from sixty days to two years.

Patatas bravas: Fried, diced potatoes served with salsa brava, a spicy tomato sauce.

Pimientos de Padrón: Small green peppers from Padrón (a municipality in the province of La Coruña in the region of Galicia) that are fried in olive oil. Most are very mild, but a few in each batch are quite spicy.

Pulpo: Octopus, typically served in small chunks and lightly salted.

Queso con anchoas: Castilla or Manchego cheese topped with anchovies.

Rajo: Pork seasoned with garlic and parsley.

Tortilla española: A type of omelet containing fried chunks of potatoes and sometimes onion.

Zamburiñas: Spanish scallops, often served in a tomato-based sauce.

So after stuffing my face for a couple of days, one of which included a *percebes* (goose-neck barnacles) pig-out of Roman proportions at La Trainera, the best traditional seafood restaurant in Madrid, I'd worked up the stamina to eat at Casa Botín. According to Guinness World Records, Casa Botín is the oldest restaurant in the world. The restaurant is scenically located on a narrow cobblestone street about a block off the Plaza Mayor, which was the site of heresy trials and subsequent burnings during the Spanish Inquisition. Botín cooks everything over wood in the same stoves and oven that have been pumping out **suckling pigs** and lambs every day since 1725. The ancient structure houses many small dining rooms, and it shows its age with its tilted stairs, antique window casements, servers who look pulled right out of central casting, and ecstatic customers slurping down bowls of the classics: squid braised in its own ink and stewed partridge with polenta.

> A suckling pig is a piglet slaughtered between the ages of two and six weeks—before it is weaned. Suckling pig is traditionally roasted whole, and often reserved for special occasions. Next time suckling pig is on the menu, be sure to taste the skin, brains, and ears.

I spent most of my morning in the granite-floored kitchen, piling logs into the stove and cooking with the Botín employees, none of whom is younger than sixty. Hanging out in the kitchen has its perks. I scarfed down as much pig as I could handle, as well as plenty of baby *anguilas*, freshly plucked at night as they make their way up from the Sargasso Sea. The kitchen staff prepares the delicacy using a simple glazed clay pot about five inches wide, heated to 600°F. Once the pot is hot enough, they add olive oil, garlic, and a single dried hot chili. Next, they dump four or five tablespoons of these baby eels, which look a lot like vermicelli noodle pieces with eyes, into the pot and swirl the contents around with a wooden fork. By the time the dish comes to your table, the eels are cooked. It's quite a treat.

After spending some quality time in the kitchen, I headed to a **table** to enjoy my whole suckling pig. More baby pigs, which are usually under a month old or weigh less than seven pounds, are consumed in Spain than in any other place in the world. The staff there were quite proud of me; they looked on as I pried open the skull and made quick work of the ears, snout, cheeks, and brains, saving the tongue for last. Everybody in Spain eats this way, so I wasn't the only one in the dining room getting up to my elbows in pig head. Eat first, ask questions later.

 Make the floor your garbage can! It's common to throw used napkins and other waste on the floor. In fact, nine out of ten Spaniards agree that lots of trash means a good and popular bar.

Importing Iberian ham was illegal in the United States up until 2008. If you find a slab of this delicious porky goodness at your local butcher, you ought to try some. But buyer beware: at a hundred dollars a pound, *jamón ibérico* is one of the world's priciest meats.

ONE OF THE FEW REMAINING *TABERNAS*

I was in town only a few days, so, in true Spanish fashion, I headed to La Bola for a second lunch. La Bola isn't as old as Botín, but it's been open since the late nineteenth century. As I walked through its door, admiring the gorgeous woodwork and old-world leaded windows, I imagined what Madrid must have looked like two hundred years ago. The city used to be filled with *tabernas,* or taverns, somewhere in the range of eight or nine hundred. Today, they're a culturally endangered species. Only sixty or seventy *tabernas* remain, which is very sad. La Bola boasts an all-female kitchen, with a median age of seventy years. Everybody, and I mean everybody, heads there for one reason only: the legendary cocido madrileño.

Cocido madrileño is a very rich dish, and it makes for a one-pot progressive meal that every braised-food junkie needs to check out. The women start with a large decorative but highly functional clay pot, which resembles a pitcher, and fill it with lamb, pork, poultry, sausage, vegetables, and chickpeas, topping it off with a homemade broth that in and of itself makes a stunning restorative. They stack these pitchers upright, allowing them to essentially percolate on a woodburning stove for hours. Once you order your cocido, a server takes the pitcher directly from the kitchen to your table and pours the broth into a plate filled with cooked fideos, thin Spanish egg noodles a little bit thicker than angel-hair pasta. It makes a lovely soup, and you eat that part of the dish first. When you've finished your soup, they dump the smoked meats and chickpeas into the plate, serving small pots of sea salt, pickled hot peppers, and a puree of smoked and fresh peppers as condiments. Add the baskets of crusty bread to the table and you have a meal of legendary proportions.

The crew and I ended up spending the better part of the night at a restaurant that moved me like no other I've visited before or since. It was a crumbling establishment named Taberna de Antonio Sánchez, after the son of the **bullfighter** who started the restaurant in 1830. The place has been owned by a succession of bullfighters, passed down from one to the other like a family heirloom. Today, it lies in the hands of a seventy-year-old former bullfighter named Paco. Located near the Plaza de las Cortes & Huertas, at 13 Mesón de Paredes, this classic *taberna* is chock-full of bullfighting memorabilia, including the stuffed head of the animal that gored the young Sánchez.

Today bullfighting is big business in Spain, with the top matadors earning salaries comparable to those of the nation's top soccer stars and rock idols. Though the sport is a national pastime, animal rights activists are fighting to end what they deem unnecessary cruelty to animals.

For the most part, the bullfighting season in Spain runs from April until September, with most major cities having one event a week (usually on a Sunday).

A VIEW OF HISTORY

Paco showed me around the tavern, pointing out the tables where famous writers like Ernest Hemingway had come to eat, drink, and write late into the evening. The décor in this place is all original—tables, chairs, and even the wineglasses. They still use the ancient dumbwaiters, as well as the old kegs where they store the famous Valdepeñas wine the *taberna* was renowned for, and still serves. Paco led me by the hand to the dark-paneled walls where three unique works by the famed Spanish artist Zuloaga still hang. Zuloaga had his last public exhibition in this restaurant.

Nothing has really changed over the years: the zinc countertops on the bars are still in use, photographs of old-time bullfighters like the legendary Frascuelo or Lagartijo still hang on the walls. The marble pedestal tables are the ones where the authors of the Generation of '98—the group of creative writers, born in the 1870s, who are known best for their criticism of the Spanish literary and educational establishments and whose major works fall in the two decades after 1898—argued late into the night. There are still the crumbling old posters advertising "torrijas"—the equivalent of American French toast—for fifteen cents or warning customers that spitting on the floor is forbidden.

After the tour, we pulled up a stiff, rickety seat at a small table in the corner to enjoy a house specialty. Bulls are revered not just in the *taberna*'s décor and history, but on the menu as well. Callos, a casserole made with blood sausage and tripe, is a traditional comfort food of Spain. This version was unlike any I've experienced—so rich and sticky and filled with so much collagen that if you kept your mouth closed too long, your lips would actually stick together. Just like the history and décor, the dish was absolutely incredible. We ate chipirónes en su tinta, which are tiny squid cooked in their own ink, and other classic dishes that the restaurant has been serving almost without exception since the day it opened for business: stewed snails, San Isidro omelet, bacalao with onions, fried eggs on a bed of crisped potatoes, and the famous oxtail stew.

Now, if only the Taberna de Antonio Sánchez could attract customers. I visited it on a Thursday night. Not a soul was in the joint when we arrived, not a body came through

Whether or not you're opposed to bullfights, they do play a part in traditional Spanish culture. If you go, here's what to expect:

~First, the bull is let into the ring. The matador looks on as his assistant waves a yellow and magenta cape in front of the bull. This causes the bull to charge and allows the matador to observe the bull's demeanor.

~Then a trumpet is sounded, and picadors, a pair of horsemen, jab the bull with a lance. This is intended to straighten the bull's charge, weaken the animal, and lower his head for the next phase of the fight.

~At this point, the matador takes over. He begins his *faena,* the series of passes performed prior to killing the bull. The matador carries a muleta—a piece of crimson cloth hung from a stick, which both encourages the bull to charge and obscures the matador's sword. The bull repeatedly charges the matador in this dramatic dance with death: One wrong move and the matador becomes a human kebab. The *faena* continues until the matador proves his superiority over the bull. Once that is accomplished, the bull is to be killed.

~The matador stands ten feet from the bull, keeping it fixated on the muleta. The matador then attacks the bull, pushing his sword over the horns and deep between the shoulder blades. This is intended to sever the bull's spinal cord, causing the animal to drop to its knees and die.

~The matador receives flowers from the crowd and is given trophies from the animal—often the ears, the tail, and a hoof.

the door the entire two hours we were there. It was down-right depressing. The streets around the *taberna* used to bustle with activity; now, too narrow for most cars to navigate, they lay silent. This used to be the neighborhood where bullfighters came to see and be seen; now, they're regarded as rock stars, touring the Costa Brava on ostentatious yachts with their supermodel girlfriends. Additionally, the food that Paco serves is not as popular as it once was. The restaurant seems doomed.

But Paco soldiers on, showing up every day to make the best callos in Madrid, giving anyone who will listen a history lesson from a guy who lived and loved in a way that doesn't exist in today's disposable pop culture world.

FORGOTTEN FOODS: JUICY CHEESE WORMS ARE MAKING A COMEBACK!

Running all over the world, hunting bats in Samoa, fishing with a Sicilian family, cooking donkey in a restaurant in Beijing—trying to experience food and share culture can lead you into some lonely territory. I often find myself spending time with folks living on the verge of cultural extinction, which can get downright depressing. However, the great thing about traveling is that for every sad story I unveil and undoubtedly sit with for a while, I find another person, ingredient, or culinary tradition that is all about revival and redemption.

My recent trip to **Nicaragua** was all about this positive spirit, reminding me of the National Geographic documentaries I used to watch as a kid. I'd be mesmerized by the schools of salmon swimming upstream to spawn at the top of

Nicaragua is Central America's largest country and is bordered by Honduras to the north and Costa Rica to the south.

our Northwestern river systems. Without fail, there is always that last fish you're not sure will make it, and the cameras always made a point of telling his story. If you're anything like me, you're always rooting for that fish. Nicaragua, despite a century of constant struggles and hardships, is finally reaching the top of that proverbial stream.

Nicaragua is an overlooked destination for travelers, to say the least. Roughly the size of New York State, the country boasts two huge freshwater lakes, Managua and Nicaragua, as well as ocean borders to the east and west. In fact, it's believed the name Nicaragua means "surrounded by water" and stems from one of the many indigenous languages. The country is visually stunning and scenic, with tropical lowlands, sandy beaches, and narrow coastal plains interrupted by volcanoes. Hundreds of small islands and cays lie on the eastern shores, providing some of the best "let's get lost" islands in Central America.

A LITTLE HISTORY . . .

In 1972, a massive earthquake destroyed the downtown in the nation's capital, Managua. Much of what had been there needed to be rebuilt in a new location. The old downtown is nearly deserted. The businesses all moved, so the residential area around the old city center is nearly abandoned. The old presidential palace, Hall of the People, and the national museum are overrun by squatters. Nobody thinks it's safe. So with the new city that was erected five miles away, it's sort of an odd town, missing a vibrant cultural center. Additionally, the area has been plagued by hurricanes, most recently 1998's Hurricane Mitch, which devastated the country.

The people of Nicaragua experienced a huge political transformation as well. Although Nicaragua declared independence from Spain in 1821, it wasn't able to stand on its own two feet until recently. The country was mostly ruled by the Spanish elite until the Sandinista Revolution in 1979, which resulted in a short-lived civil war that brought a committed band of Marxist Sandinista guerrillas to power. Although the country's free elections in 1990, 1996, and 2001 all defeated the Sandinistas, it wasn't until Daniel Ortega's reelection in 2006 that the country could seriously start **rebuilding.** Nicaragua seems well on its way to greatness. I'm just keeping my fingers crossed that there are no more natural disasters, no more revolutions for a while, and that Nicaragua will get a chance to bloom on its own.

> **╫┃●** Nicaragua has the lowest crime rate in Central America. It is also the second-poorest country in the Western Hemisphere, after Haiti.

What I love about this country is that despite the hardships, earthquakes, storms, and revolutions, Nicaraguans are some of the most resilient, kind, caring, and open people I've met. They are for the most part poor, and yet everyone shares everything with guests. On my first day there, I met up with Sergio Zepeda in his small town of Masaya. He's a guitar maker now, but he used to be a famous musician in a boy band, sort of like the Nicaraguan Menudo.

Sergio asks if I've had a chance to eat the iguana eggs. I haven't, so he leads me over to a table tended by a crone with three bowls in front of her, each filled with a light tomato porridge. Floating in the bowl are a dozen small golf-ball-size eggs. The embryo is encased in a soft, fibrous shell that you bite into before you suck out the contents. A horrific methodology, but pretty darn tasty. Very much like a chicken egg, but smaller and with a thinner, metallic flavor.

A DELICIOUS RIDE

I spent the next day on a bus from Managua to Estelí, a town high up in the mountains. You catch the bus at Mayoreo Market, roughly ten minutes from the airport. The buses are big American-style school buses, circa 1968, and I finally selected mine, a shimmering red-and-silver beast named Tranquilo No. 7. Every bus has a slick name. Before we hopped on our selected bus, we picked up some nut brittle from one of the hawkers, then set out on the Gringo Trail and headed north on the Pan-American Highway.

I quickly discovered that a lengthy Nicaraguan bus ride is like a mobile progressive meal. Every time we stopped, kids and older men rushed onto the bus carrying pieces of fruit, chopped watermelon, doughnuts, whatever it might be. By the time you reach your destination, you're stuffed. We ate quesillo, a white cheese served in a plastic bag with vinegar chilies and tortilla, as well as cuajada, a curdled cheese made at a farm on a hill high above the highway. My favorite dish was vigorón. It was shredded cabbage topped with pork cracklings and dressed with lime and orange juice and bits of sliced tomatoes. It was fresh and crunchy, and it totally hit the spot after I had spent the day in a hot bus. After disembarking, I wandered around Estelí, checking out the amazing produce market there.

Later, I hooked up with a pal who lives in the area. We hung out in Estelí for a while, eventually making our way north into the foothills of the Cloud Forest. We stopped at a truck-stop place called Don Juan Papaya's for a little bowl of soup, and a short while later at Antojitos, where I met some of my friend's Peace Corps buddies. We ate some grilled armadillo and grilled boa constrictor in a restaurant that specializes in this local fare; the food was superb, and I was full.

A PERFECT CUP OF COFFEE

We spent that evening at a place called Selva Negra, an old coffee plantation turned eco-hotel. The howler monkeys kept me up most of the night, but it was worth it to wake up in absolutely stunning surroundings, with a dense tropical rain forest high above the hot plains. We finished the drive to Matagalpa that morning to hit the Sol Café. If you're a coffee connoisseur, add a visit to Sol Café in Matagalpa to your bucket list. The coffee business in Nicaragua is fascinating. Here is a food item representative of the campesinos' years of struggle against oppressors who've exploited their livelihood. However, like the rest of the country, this industry is bouncing back.

The Thanksgiving Coffee Company, which operates out of the Sol Café, is a conglomerate of hundreds of local farmers, some of whom have only a few acres of trees to pick beans from. As a co-op, they sell to coffee companies all over the world. Starbucks, Newman's Own—you name it, they're buying coffee from Thanksgiving Coffee. The coffee association hired tasters and blenders to help craft a signature coffee style from beans that hail from different farms. When you see how slick and innovative this system is, you become a believer. This is going to work. They are a fair-trade coffee company and they receive a fair market price for their goods. A certain percentage from each sale goes to civic works projects such as local clinics or helping rebuild schools. We toured the facility at Sol Café, where local farmers bring their beans to be dried in the sun, graded again, and bagged for selling. Hundreds of laborers work in superb conditions, with benefits, and earn about 20 percent more in their pocket than at other agrarian enterprises in Matagalpa. It's a really positive story, and just more proof that Nicaragua is a turn-around country.

TO THE BLUEFIELDS

One of the great experiences along those lines came the next day when we flew to Bluefields, located on the Atlantic coast of Nicaragua. Bluefields is a Creole community, where everyone speaks English with a pronounced Creole lilt. And since there are no roads to the area, Bluefields is cut off from the rest of the country. You can get there only by boat from another port or by taking the one plane a day that stops in the teeny town on its way to Corn Island, a tropical paradise popular with the beach freaks. We spent the night in a hotel above a casino and journeyed the next day to the home of

Edna Cayasso, a local grandma who specializes in the traditional Atlantic coast cuisine developed by the first Africans in Bluefields.

Edna, her three sons, and the sons' wives and kids all live in one building, with Edna still ruling the kitchen. During our visit, she made rondón, a traditional Creole dish called "rundown" in Creole communities outside of Spanish-speaking countries. Rondón is a melding of flavors and cultures—born in Africa, filtered through flavors of the Caribbean, and now treasured by small communities who have eaten it for generations. It's a thick stew of meat, vegetables, and coconut milk, sturdy with sweet potatoes, plantains, yucca, and starchy tubers called cocos, which remind me of a cross between a cassava and a potato. The ingredients are thrown into a bowl filled with water. As far as protein goes, Edna opted for a chopped, browned wari, which is essentially a wild jungle rat that resembles a peccary. The starches and meat absorb the liquid as it cooks, resulting in a dish as delicious as it is diverse.

Rondón is the quintessential Nicaraguan Creole food, and it is something that people like Edna Cayasso revere as more of a tradition than a simple dish. It's apparent that passing her passion for Creole cuisine on to the next generation is a high priority, as she insists her whole family make the dish together.

She served the rondón with coconut rice and beans, coconut bread, and two homemade beverages made from cassava and seaweed. These drinks are called "seaweed pop" and "cassava pop." The seaweed pop was crafted from a puree of local seaweed, rehydrated with water, and seasoned with nutmeg. It's more of a sludge than anything else. I politely accepted the nearly undrinkable beverage, but in my head I wanted to run screaming from the table.

Fun Spanish Food Phrases

Tengo hambre. I'm hungry.

¡Buen provecho! Enjoy your meal!

¿Puedo probarlo? Can I have a bite of that?

Quiero dos tacos de lengua. I'll take two beef tongue tacos.

Pareceria bien si, tomarlo. If it looks good, eat it.

¡Como gelatinoso! How gelatinous!

Es rancio. It's rancid.

On our last day, I had the ultimate uplifting food experience I'd been hoping for in this country of redemptive experiences. We traveled south to Granada, a city where everything comes together—the Pacific, North, Central, and Atlantic regions—both in the people's food and in their heritage. Granada is a colonial Spanish town that in many ways has remained unchanged for hundreds of years.

You can climb to the top of the church's bell tower and look out over the rooftops. It's a sea of gorgeous curved clay-tiled roofs, not an antenna or satellite dish in sight. The smell of cooking fires wafts through the streets. It's an absolutely charming place, with artisanal chocolate shops, and cozy city parks teeming with visitors and performance artists everywhere you look. The narrow cobblestone streets are a challenge to navigate, only because you spend the whole time craning your neck gazing at all the stunning Spanish Colonial architecture. We were there the night of a big poetry and arts festival, where I had the pleasure of meeting the Nicaraguan vice president as well as a bunch of local dignitaries.

I ended my night at a sleepy little restaurant and hotel where, I admit, my expectations were low. At first glance, Casa San Francisco, a quaint, family-run hotel about three blocks off the main square, was nothing special. However, once I entered the ancient courtyard, I changed my tune. Quiet and beautiful, with a plunge pool surrounded by bougainvillea, the place just had that old Spanish western feel. Upon learning of my arrival, chefs Octavio Gomez and Vernon Hodgson went out of their way to up the ante a little in the kitchen. Vernon decided to reinvent a few rural dishes and raise them up on the altar.

TRADITIONAL DISHES OF GRANADA

They kicked off dinner with historical local fruit flavors, serving a platter of nispero, pera de agua, green mangoes, and star fruit. We washed that course down with a batido, a sapote fruit milk shake. The main dish was quintessentially Nicaraguan with a modern twist—wild iguana, marinated in sour orange, cumin, achiote, and garlic. They roasted the lizard whole, crisping the skin just like duck à l'orange—it was outstanding.

Aged Chontales cheese was the real star of the meal. It's a small wheel of soft, Muenster-like cheese, served in the ancient style of the Caribbean coast. You allow the cheese to age in the heat of the day, just long enough to produce large maggots. When you open the cheese, these juicy cheese worms, as they call them, are then eaten right along with the cheese, just hundreds of these suckers wriggling on the end of your knife. It's one of the most horrific and wonderful things I have ever seen on a plate.

The worm origin somehow remains a mystery, scientifically speaking. But I did manage to get the cultural story. One of the chefs explained that the cheese process originates from the time of the very first Sandinista National Liberation Front. During that period, people near the front wouldn't throw away old cheese because it was so difficult to obtain any food at all in that time of war. Instead, they let the cheese ferment, hanging it in a sack to eliminate the *suero*, or whey, from the fresh cheese. Once the cheese lost its liquid, it began the process of decomposition. It's at that time that the cheese develops the worms, which continue to grow as long as you let the cheese ferment. Some people remove the worms and eat them fried; others eat them in their natural state.

The whole idea of eating maggot-laden cheese is enough to boggle most anyone's mind, but what I couldn't shake is the idea that a traditional food like worm-filled Chontales cheese has been eradicated from this part of Nicaragua. Octavio admitted he's been clueless on how to make it, consulting aged family members to resurrect the delicacy. The cheese wasn't a dying breed—it was already dead and in the ground. When the chef learned I was coming to town, he saw the perfect opportunity to re-create this cheese for an audience that might actually enjoy eating it.

He started out with fresh country cheese, queso casero or queso creolo. (It's important that you use raw-milk products from rural areas, because dairy products in the city use too much scientific methodology to kill the bacteria and avoid decomposition.) He crafted a basket of plantain leaves, hanging the fresh cheese from it for three days to remove the *suero*. Next, he rolled the cheese in fresh plantain leaves to hold its shape. Once the cheese begins to decompose, flies will lay their eggs in the rotting matter. On the seventh day, the cheese starts producing eggs, which resemble fine grains of rice. It takes an additional twenty-four hours to hatch the worms. Luis served it to me four days later, which allowed the worms to grow to quite a decent size.

Although nature does much of the work for you, it takes a lot of patience to stick out the two-week-long decomposition period. That, in addition to the fact that the cheese tastes like a rotten-foot bomb went off in your mouth, has a lot to do with its phasing out. The cheese flavor is strong and pungent—something I adore. It reminded me of the washed-rind cheese Stinking Bishop, which I eat whenever I can find some, but this one has the bonus of the wriggling worms busting out of it. Suffice to say, there's not a big market for Chontales cheese riddled with maggots, despite the desirable protein in those worms. And the process can goof up on you if the cheese doesn't lose its liquid. If that happens, the flavor will be kept even more rotten and putrefied and you can't eat it. So there is a very fine balance here. This isn't *Fear Factor* food, this is good cooking.

The most disgusting-looking food is often the best-tasting. As foul an idea as it is to shove a runny, smelly *fromage,* riddled with something you'd rather bait a fishing hook with, into your mouth, it was pretty darn tasty. Eating outside your comfort zone allows you to acknowledge the baggage that you carry into each meal, that evil corruptive contempt prior to investigation, which thankfully can disappear pretty quickly.

WELCOME TO A WAZWAN:
THE MEAL THAT NEARLY KILLED ME

One of the best meals of my life happened to take the longest to eat. It was also the meal that began the latest in the evening and finished the earliest in the morning. To get the full picture of it, we have to backtrack.

India, much like its food, is complex and full of contrasts. Its capital city of Delhi perfectly exemplifies this, as it is gritty and ugly, yet simultaneously elegant. It's modern and ancient, affluent and poor. It's a city of Hindu and Sikh temples and red clay mosques. There is poverty and sickness. There are beggars in the streets, and there are serene parks and gorgeous architecture. Delhi has more than 13 million people, making it the second-largest city in India. There are dozens of indigenous ethnic groups and religious cultures. From some of the best restaurants in the world to humble everyday cafés, you can find every one of the many Indian cuisines represented in Delhi. Fortunately, I had the opportunity to dive mouth first into several.

VISITING DELHI

Delhi is the oldest continuously lived-in city in the world, going back at least twenty-five hundred years. The ruins of seven other cities have been discovered on the site, and it is said that Delhi's food scene can be traced to its medieval inhabitants. Today Shahjahanabad, or Old Delhi, is home to an army of office workers and of shopkeepers who trade in everything from spices to tapestries, bridal treasures to electrical fittings. If you venture through the tangle of streets and dark alleys into busy boulevards, you are likely to find surprises lurking around the corner, especially when it comes to street food.

Traditional street foods are continuously bulldozed under in a busy, hectic city like Delhi. But you can find cold, spiced frothed milk; tiny stands that serve nahari—a spicy, curried lamb dish; and vendors selling fruit puree sandwiches. I explored Chawri Bazaar and sampled all these goodies there. Food and eating are a strong element of every Indian culture. Interestingly, the one thing that brings most people together in most parts of the world is often what keeps people apart in India. Culture and religion in India segregate people, especially when it comes to food. Some eat meat. Some won't even allow meat inside their homes. Some fast in order to be closer to God; others say fasting is the path to weakness and is therefore evil.

EATING EQUALITY

I visited one place, however, where all cultures, all religions, all walks of life can sit down side by side and share a meal: the Langar of the Gurdwara Bangla Sahib, also known as the Kitchen of the Sikh Temples. Sikh culture promotes nonviolence and vegetarianism. Sikhs are strong believers in Karma and attribute karmic values to everything they do, including the air they breathe, the water they use, and the light of the sun and moon, as well as the food they eat. Around the world, the Sikhs are known for treating all people as equals. This ideology is embodied in the two daily meals served at Gurdwara Bangla Sahib, where anyone can volunteer to cook in the *langar*, or community kitchen, and people of every race and religion are welcome to eat free of charge. Between eight and nine thousand visitors are served daily, with no division between a lunch and a dinner hour. It's always mealtime at the *langar*, and everyone who enters understands that the food is a gift from God.

The food served at the temple is by no means fancy, consisting of basic staples: dahl, a spicy dish made from lentils, tomatoes, and onions; roti, an unleavened griddle-baked flatbread; and curried vegetables. I helped roll out roti and then stew the dahl and vegetables, which went on to feed thousands of my newest friends. Literally sharing food and culture. It was quite fantastic, although, I must admit, I was glad to be exempted from dishwashing duty.

Interestingly, a simple ingredient has the ability to bridge the gap between religious and cultural groups. Where religions demand adherence to exclusive diets, milk is one of the only items common in homes across India. To the Hindus, who make up more than 80 percent of the Indian population, the **cow** is revered as sacred. Thus milk is a sacred ingredient, often used not only in food but for spiritual cleansing purposes as well. Believe it or not, India is the largest producer of milk in the world.

From main dishes to specialty drinks, milk plays a huge role in Indian cooking. Not all Delhiies are comfortable with the suspect processed version that you and I buy at the supermarket. Instead, they rely on fresh milk from the cows down the street—and, yes, in one of the largest cities in the world, the milkman keeps his own cows in his own house and delivers milk daily. He milks the cows into large cans, hangs them on the handlebars of his scooter, and off he goes.

Kulfi, a favorite dessert of mine, is essentially the Indian ice cream; it comes in a variety of unlikely flavors, such as rosewater and saffron. The milk used in this treat is simmered down, not whipped, and the result is a solid, dense frozen dessert similar to frozen custard. We always think of Paris and Italy as the global leaders in the sweets department. Nobody ever thinks of countries like India and Japan, despite their great tradition with them.

I encountered many other unique dining traditions in the city. Old Delhi's jam-packed and bustling Nizamuddin neighborhood is the place to experience firsthand the red-meat-rich

~In Hinduism, the cow is revered as the source of food and symbol of life and may never be killed. Hindus do not worship the cow, but they do consider cows sacred.

~In honor of their exalted status, cows often roam the streets of India freely. It's considered good luck to give a cow a snack. Go with fruit—it's a bovine favorite.

~Be mindful of the cows—you can be sent to jail for killing or injuring a cow.

~A roaming cow population creates problems in densely populated cities. For instance, Delhi's 13 million residents share the streets with an estimated forty thousand cows. Cows make a mess, both with their dung and by spreading trash in the city streets as they dig through garbage searching for discarded food. Of course, they can also act as a living, slow-moving roadblock, creating major traffic jams.

~Forget about diamonds, gold, or cold hard cash. The cow is still the most highly regarded gift in rural India.

~Consuming beef or veal is considered sacrilegious for Hindus. Slaughter of cows is illegal in almost all the states of the Indian Union. McDonald's restaurants in India serve only vegetable, chicken, or fish burgers.

Muslim cuisine (they typically opt for buffalo). In Delhi's largest Muslim mosque, I indulged in nayaab maghz masala, mutton brain cooked with cheese curds and curry. They're also well-known for kalije, which is a savory liver and kidney stew; gurda kapura, chopped kidneys and testicles; and nalli nihari, a spicy stew made with buffalo marrow and buffalo feet and skin.

And then there is Bengali cuisine, which hails from India's northeastern state of West Bengal. The culinary traditions there are founded on the rich selection of grains, seafood, bananas, and spices, primarily a customized blend of nigella, black mustard, fenugreek, fennel, and cumin seeds. I visited one of Delhi's newer neighborhoods, Nehru Place, where I had the pleasure of cooking lunch with chef Joy Banerjee. Joy is an expert on Bengali food and specializes in re-creating family recipes of a bygone era. He mans the kitchen at Oh! Calcutta, named after the avant-garde British musical from the 1970s.

Cooking lunch with Joy turned into one of the best eating experiences of my journey. The banana is extremely popular in Bengali cuisine, mostly because it's convenient and abundant. Additionally, every part of the plant—flower to trunk—is edible. After watching the complex preparation of each banana specialty, I feasted on Bengali dishes like sautéed tree trunks, fish bathed in mustard oil and wrapped in banana leaves, and mochar ghonts, a dish featuring foot-long banana flowers.

In addition to offering some amazing street food and wonderful cafés, Delhi houses some of the best fine dining in the world. Bukhara, a tandoori eatery *Restaurant* magazine has often proclaimed as the best restaurant in Asia, is one such place. It's a see-and-be-seen favorite of rock stars, presidents, and royalty. The food is exquisite. The tandoori is beyond compare, and I've eaten tandoori in the best street stalls and most elegant restaurants in the world. Bukhara does simple tandoori cooking better than anybody—it's magical. What's more, the casual atmosphere in a place as renowned as Bukhara is rather bizarre. Patrons are urged to eat not with silverware but with their **hands.** In fact, the chef insists on it,

Posing with my dinner—a boa constrictor—in Nicaragua.
Due to the large number of bones in the snake, this dish is best
eaten with your fingers. It's surprisingly delicious!

Roasting whole *cuy*, or guinea pig, with my friend Martha at Fiambre's in Mitad del Mundo, Ecuador. Eating guinea pig sounds weird at first, but the meat is very tender and falls right off the bone!

About to nosh at a raw meat stand in Harar, Ethiopia. I'm sampling the beef here, but they also serve goat and camel.

A bowl of prepared octopus, the house specialty,
at El Grillo Marinero in La Crucecita, Mexico.

Roasted baby sparrows at a market in Taipei, Taiwan.
You eat these things whole—bones, beak, and all!
One of my favorite snacks of all time.

Only in Japan. Massive tuna head, anyone?

Pheasant hunting just north of Edinburgh, Scotland.

Snorkeling off the remote island of Nu'utele, Samoa. These waters are so thick with tuna, some Samoans actually use it as currency.

Reading production notes during some downtime on location in Tanzania. One of my favorite photos from *Bizarre Foods.*

At Maketi Fou Market in Samoa with a mouthful of *se'e*—sea slug
guts bottled in seawater. I can best describe *se'e* as
stringy, salty, and rotten tasting, and not in a good way.

Attending meat camp (where men gather and eat as much meat as they can for five days) with the Masai tribe of Tanzania was one of the greatest experiences of my life.

claiming it enhances the whole eating experience, giving diners a deeper connection to the food.

THE FEAST OF ALL FEASTS

However, no single experience can compare to the deeply complex and lavish meal I had with a group of Kashmiri hipsters. Food in the Indian state of Kashmir isn't just about eating, it's an all-sensory sacred tradition. Kashmiri cuisine is as much about art and style and ritual as it is about the food. I've met Kashmiris while growing up in New York, traveling through India, and even living in Minnesota, where I've been based for nearly eighteen years. Without question, these folks are some of the most outgoing and outrageous personalities I've ever met. They are all about the party. That boisterous quality is not very surprising, considering that the state was a big hub for every spice and silk route that you have ever seen on an ancient map. Persian, Afghan, and Central Asian merchants passed through the area, and while for many it was just a stop along the way, their influence stuck with the Kashmiri people.

Kashmiri dining traditions are lavish, with an obvious passion for **hospitality.** Traditionally, the Kashmiri host lays out all the food that he has at home before his guests. Then

> If you're not Indian, be prepared for the locals to stare intensely at you. This isn't considered rude; they're just curious and interested in who you are and where you came from. Often, people (even complete strangers) will ask you very personal questions—about your age, income, appearance, and health. While it might feel invasive at first, it provides a great opportunity to ask them about their lives.

the guests fulfill their role by grazing on the abundant spread until the food has disappeared. And thus the *wazwan* feast was born. A *wazwan* meal can consist of as many as forty courses. Organizing this meal is not for the faint of heart (nor is eating it, as I soon found out). Not only must the host select the numerous courses, he or she must also be willing to perform certain traditional ceremonies that accompany each dish.

Leave it to renowned Kashmiri fashion designer Rohit Bal to take on the daunting task of creating one seriously over-the-top *wazwan* feast. These meals often entail many days of preparation and hours of cooking. I received the invite the first night that I landed in Delhi. And while I was completely wiped from traveling, I could not resist the opportunity to hang with this guy. I couldn't think of a better host for this kind of spirited feast, which is typically for special occasions and weddings these days. The colorful meal is a ritual, the preparation of which is considered an art form. The chefs, who are called *wazas*, pass this trade on through the apprentice system, from chef to chef to chef. While the traditional number of courses is thirty-six, there are sometimes a few more or less, and the preparation is traditionally done by the *vasta waza*, or head chef, with the assistance of *wazas*.

I arrived at Rohit's home, located in one of the glitzier sections of Delhi. His neighborhood is absolutely beautiful, complete with parks and oversize three- and four-story brownstone homes. Rohit lives on the top floor of one of these gorgeous buildings. Even though it was ten p.m., I was one of the first guests to arrive. As I entered Rohit's home, I could smell food coming from all over the place, but, curiously, his kitchen was empty. Apparently, the *wazas* had spent the previous twenty-four hours cooking, chopping, dicing, pureeing, boiling, sautéing, and baking in the hallways of his building. They arrive with pots and pan, burners and bowls, cutting boards and curios, and they take over.

Waz Up with the *Wazwan* Dinner?

~This dinner is truly a meat lover's paradise. Most of the courses are made with a variety of meats, like lamb, mutton (sheep), chicken, and beef, and also fish.

~Sharing food at the table is the focus of a *wazwan* dinner. In fact, guests sit on the floor in groups of four to six around a metal plate (*trami*) and often eat with their hands. Don't worry, though, a hand-washing ceremony takes place at the start of dinner. Whatever you do, don't eat with your left hand.

~ *"Vasta waza"* means "chief cook," and usually this person has inherited his culinary skills from a long line of *waza* family members. He spends days preparing for the meal and assists his team with the food before the ceremony.

~Tea is an important part of the Kashmiri culture and the *wazwan* dinner. It's said to rejuvenate the body.

~With more than forty courses to the meal, it's likely your host will send you home with a doggie bag—especially after a wedding.

So there I was. I was nervous. I mean, I didn't know anyone at the party. There were models, filmmakers, TV news anchors, and other Indian celebrities, and they all looked so fabulous. In no time, the Kashmiri knack for hospitality kicked in and the evening ended up being a real learning experience in Indian high society.

After about an hour and a half, we finally sat down for dinner. Rohit had cleared out his entire living room and outfitted it with bright lights and a Kashmiri silk carpet. Everyone was seated on the floor, in groups of three or four, on top of gorgeous pillows set in a semicircle, and that was where we began with the first ritual of the evening. A *tash-t-nari*, an ornate silver basin, was passed by the attendants for guests to wash their hands. This ritual is less about hygiene than it is about symbolizing the cleansing of the soul and ridding yourself of negative energies.

Next, large serving dishes arrived. These were piled high with heaps of rice, and divided into four quadrants with seekh kebabs, which are made up of meat sausages that have been skewered and grilled. It's perfect for this kind of shared meal—four guests get to eat off the same plate, but everyone has his or her own personal zone. Four portions of different types of purees and yogurt sauces and sides of barbecued lamb ribs sit in the platter as well. The meal is accompanied by yogurt that is garnished with Kashmiri saffron and different salads and pickles and dips, and you just kind of start eating the moment the food arrives.

One of the cornerstones of the *wazwan* is making a whole lamb part of the process, ensuring that every part of the lamb is utilized. More than thirty varieties of lamb are raised in that part of the world, and this multicourse meal makes use of the animal in nearly every dish. It's even considered a sacrilege in some serious Kashmiri homes to serve at the feast any dishes that are based on lentils or grains. We were offered handfuls of fried lamb ribs sprinkled with turmeric, chilies, and lime juice. The dish was deliciously fatty and rich, which from a flavor standpoint I absolutely love. However, after two or three of these mini racks of ribs I was almost full. At that point, it was nearly midnight and I was ready to go to sleep. But the next thing you know, more food starts pouring in.

Every time you'd finished a course, more food would arrive. Fried lotus stems. Cottage cheese squares. Bowls of chilies and radishes and walnut chutney. A parade of four or five different stewed lamb dishes, one after another after another. Lamb curry cooked in milk. Jellied bouillon made from the meat and bones. Eggplant and apple stew. Rogan josh, a very spicy lamb stew. Another lamb stew made with tree resin. Mustard oil–based roast lamb. Cockscombs. Saffron-infused lamb. But the highlight was gushtaba. Food books describe them as balls of chopped lamb seasoned with spices and cooked in oil, milk, and curds. That doesn't even begin to describe the process. The chefs put raw lamb, a bit of garlic, and some mild spices in a mortar and begin to pound the mixture with a pestle, adding handfuls of minced fat as they go. It takes on the texture of a hot dog and it tastes like bologna, but like the best lamb bologna you ever ate. So light, with so much fat beaten into it. It holds a ball shape, so you can cut it with a knife, and even though it has a hot-dog-like chew to it, it also has this melting, smooth quality—

it disappears down your throat as quickly as you're chewing it. It's one of the most glorious dishes I have ever tasted.

We had thirty-six courses, and finally, at two-thirty in the morning, I needed to be thrown in a wheelbarrow and rolled back to the hotel. I was the first to arrive and I was also the first to leave. Despite the warnings to slow down and not eat it all at once, I pushed the pedal to the metal. You have to pace yourself. The food tasted unlike anything I've had before, and I probably will never experience it again. Holding back is way too tall an order for someone like me.

And so I wandered out to the streets of Delhi looking for a cab, desperate for a few hours to lie down to try and digest this amazing meal. Nobody loves lamb more than I do, but the next day, I swore to myself, I am never eating lamb again. I had lamb fat coming out of my pores for days. Of course, with such an amazing array of lamb dishes available in that city, it was only a matter of time before I caved on that one.

Mary's Corner: The Quest for the Best Laksa in Singapore

Most Americans think they know what characteristics make for the best hot dog. Some say it's all about the sauerkraut or relish. Others think it's Heinz ketchup and yellow mustard. And then there is that group of people who believe one drop of the fancy red or yellow stuff completely ruins a tube steak. But at least we can all agree that encased ground meat served on a bun is the foundation for a basic hot dog.

Well, laksa is to parts of Southeast Asia what hot dogs are to America. This dish is one of the most popular soups served in that region, especially Singapore, Malaysia, and Indonesia. There are many different styles of preparation, and everyone has an opinion about what makes one bowl better than another. Laksa is a spicy noodle soup that originated in the Peranakan culture, a heritage often referred to as Baba-Nyonya. As a group, the Peranakans formed centuries ago when indigenous Malays merged with some of the descendants of Chinese immigrants.

Many different dishes symbolize Peranakan culture, most notably otak-otak, a sausage made of ground and seasoned forcemeat and steamed in thin portions in bamboo, banana, or other edible leaves. It can also be grilled or baked. To some people this is the most popular and iconic of all the traditional Peranakan foods, but my favorite regional dish is laksa.

To understand this dish is to understand two things: One, it's an easy, cheap meal in a bowl, with lots of noodles and shellfish in the broth. Malays, Singaporeans, and Southeast Asian food freaks argue about what makes for authentic and honest laksa. To me, that sort of culinary dialogue often misses the point. You can argue about whether or not crispy shallots belong on top, or whether little strings of cold omelet should be julienned and stirred in, or how thick the broth should be— whether it should be thin and sour (as it often is in Thailand) or thick, rich, and creamy with a sturdy foundation of coconut milk. And let's not even get started on noodle options. Who cares? All those soups belong in the laksa family. It's like arguing over pizza. It doesn't really matter whether it's from a grocer's freezer or a neighborhood wood-fired-oven joint, it's all pizza as long as it tastes good to someone.

OFF TO FIND THE BEST

I've often thought that what propelled laksa to such incredible heights can largely be attributed to the jump in American tourism over the last forty or fifty years, where visitors came back to their hometowns raving about the best meal-in-a-bowl. The obsession with this high-energy, big-flavor dish reached staggering proportions because the combination of flavors is just simply off the charts. Any traveler who goes to Singapore and doesn't have a bowl of laksa might as well call the trip a waste of time. Once you have tried it, you become consumed with it.

I'd been dying to get to Singapore for as long as I can remember, and finally had my chance in 2008. On most trips, the first impression of a country comes as your plane prepares for landing. Sometimes it's what you see through the window; other times it's what you hear over the intercom. This is especially pertinent when landing in Singapore. It is a kindly auditory welcome mat stating, "It is ninety-eight degrees Fahrenheit, thirty-four degrees Celsius, this morning in Singapore. Please mind overhead compartments, as luggage items may have shifted during flight. And please remember that swearing and spitting on the ground are against the law, and the use or importation of illegal drugs, even for personal consumption, is punishable by death." It's the kind of thing that makes you gasp the first time you hear it.

A FEW OF THE FACTS

The Republic of Singapore is certainly a unique place. It's a very small island, roughly four times the size of Washington, D.C., with about five million inhabitants. Singapore is one of few city-states in the world. There is Monaco and there is Vatican City, which are certainly rarefied company. Singapore, which boasts a gorgeous natural harbor with very deep water, is strategically positioned in the Pacific Ocean among the low-hanging Southeast Asian countries. Take a look at a map and you can see why this was the perfect place for the British East India Company to send one of their most aggressive agents, a gentleman named Sir Thomas Stamford Raffles.

Sir Thomas arrived on the island to create a British trade port that was intended to compete with the Dutch, who were Europe's big trading force in the region. He founded the city of Singapore in 1819, and it became a British colony. Subsequently, it joined the Federation of Malaysia in 1963, and then became an independent republic in 1965. Currently, Singapore is populated predominantly by people of Chinese extraction, who make up 76 percent of the total population. Another 15 percent or so are the indigenous Malay people, and about 8 percent are Indians.

I was surprised to discover that Indians made up such a small percentage of the Singaporean population, given that Indian culture in Singapore is so vibrant and quite predominant. You can't turn around in the street without seeing the wide sway of Indian influence. Considering the country's diverse cultural makeup, it's easy to see how—and I admit, I hate this term—one of the world's most famously original "fusion" cuisines was born here. English, Dutch, and European influence on a Chinese and Malay culture, with free-flowing Indian exposure, spices, food styles, curries—this is the stuff that creates the ultimate hybrid food palette.

Eating has become a national pastime in this modern, bustling country. People eat all day long, and so my first job was to find out where most people do their chowing down. My priority was to check out the hawker centers, and I do love street food. I think that's the best way to eat, because you have so many options. Some stalls are more like restaurants, offering five or six dishes, while others specialize in one dish, like barbecued ribs, stewed mutton, or otak-otak.

GOING FROM STALL TO STALL

I was ecstatic to visit People's Park, which boasts hundreds of stalls. I also checked out the Zion Riverside Food Centre, as well as Adam Road Food Centre, which is in a Muslim neighborhood, so all the food there is halal. People's Park is the one that I returned to on several occasions—it doesn't hurt that it's right in the center of town.

Many Americans get flustered in hawker stall environments in foreign countries, freaking out about whether or not they'll be hovering over a toilet for hours after having a few bites of street food. I wouldn't stress too much about that in Singapore. These hawker centers are spotless. Singapore has a well deserved reputation for strict laws (I mean, they outlaw *chewing gum*), so the extreme cleanliness of the country is not surprising. This is a country in pursuit of excellence. They want to be the best when it comes to food. They want to be the most crime-free country on the planet. They want to be the cleanest city in the world.

Given some of the places I visit and the things I eat on *Bizarre Foods*, it might surprise you that cleanliness around food is extremely important to me. Not just from a visual standpoint—I actually get concerned about my well-being when I see a lot of filth and degradation. That's no environment to be preparing food in. Sadly, that's how much of the

Singapore is known for enforcing some pretty strange laws. For example:

~Bungee jumping is illegal.

~Selling gum, as well as chewing it, will land you a hefty fine.

~You may not walk around in your home nude.

~Spitting, littering, smoking in public, and jaywalking are all against the law. If caught littering three times, you must clean the street while wearing a sign that states, "I am a litterer."

~Failure to flush a public toilet after use may result in a fine of up to five hundred dollars.

~It is illegal to pee in an elevator. (Okay, that one I agree with!)

~If you have a flowerpot, or anything that collects water, and mosquito larvae subsequently hatch in it, you risk being fined.

~Leave your spray paint at home—if you're caught vandalizing anything, you could get thrown in jail and caned. Caning consists of getting swatted on the bare buttocks or hands with a cane made of rattan. Yowch!

These laws seem very harsh, but, to be fair, Singapore is the cleanest country I have ever been to, and the crime rate is extremely low. Something must be working!

world operates—including the United States, which is ironically one of the filthiest food countries with respect to kitchens. Everybody hems and haws about what to eat while traveling, but I'd be more concerned about picking up a bug from something at a giant American chain restaurant than at a Singaporean hawker stall.

Hawker centers are government-run in the sense that the government owns the space and leases the stalls. This allows the government to keep the place clean and well-managed. Fortunately, the government understands that it has no business cooking food. Let the artists, the chefs, come in there and do their thing, and let them do it in an environment— the physical space—that the government maintains. The centers have tables as well as lovely little gardens where you can sit down and enjoy your food. But first you have to decide what to eat. You claim a numbered table, then walk around to the stalls that stretch for half a mile in a series of indoor and outdoor courtyards in People's Park. You order, and you let the hawkers know your table number. Once your grub is ready, a runner will ferry the food to you.

MY "STALL" SELECTIONS

I was fortunate enough to dine at People's Park the first time with Violet Oon, the Julia Child of Singapore. She was an absolutely fabulous host, and she knew her way around the Singapore food scene and was game for trying everything. We ate fantastic frog porridge and slurped pig soup filled with all the different parts of the pig: liver, heart, lungs, and so on. Grandma is in the back of the stall, stirring ten-gallon pots filled with soup made according to a generations-old family recipe. The pig soup broth base was top-heavy with sweet spices like cinnamon and star anise, ginger, lovely braised greens, and a hint of fresh lime juice to lighten it up. The soup also incorporated melting bits of braised pork rib and shoulder, and paper-thin slices of pig heart, tongue, liver, and other organs. I know that might not be up everyone's alley, but don't knock it till you try it.

Violet and I picked some dishes from a duck stall where you can get wings, tongues, split roasted heads, and sliced duck breast. We also devoured the classic Hainan chicken, which is a steamed bird that tastes like no other chicken you've placed in your mouth. It's the way chicken used to taste everywhere, I imagine, and the better hawkers purge and then gorge their birds on a diet designed to increase the brittle nature of the skin and the meat's fat content. They drizzle the cooked poultry with an aged, thickened, sweet soy

---

Andrew's Tips on Eating Street Food

~Eat local. Eating the American-style tuna salad at the hotel buffet in Marrakesh is less safe than eating the goat's head soup in the Djemma el Fna in the same city. It's a good rule of thumb to remember. In general, when you are in Beijing, don't eat the burgers at a Hard Rock Cafe. Chefs practice smarter food handling of familiar products, so in China I eat Chinese food, in Italy I eat Italian, and so on. Also, remember that going local means saving money as well.

~Follow the happy face rule. Always eat from the stand with customers, lots of happy customers (bonus points if there are lots of locals). I simply sit on a street and slow down enough to observe which places had the most diners with smiles. It's an easy trick and you'll rarely be disappointed.

~Safeguard your stomach. Eat hot food hot and cold food cold, especially in foreign countries. Food safety means more to me when traveling, when I can't afford a down day due to discomfort. Washing hands, using antibacterials, and other commonsense practices are musts.

sauce and serve it with classic Singaporean-style fried rice. People's Park was just a phenomenal experience.

Violet turned my crew and me on to a place called Tian Jin Hai Seafood Restaurant. Tian Jin Hai is the brainchild of Francis Yeo, who ran a successful seafood hawker stall for ten years.

Yeo earned a reputation for incredible chili crab at his stall. Chili crab, the Singaporean national dish, features giant mud crabs with thick shells and stout claws. He offers eight or nine different varieties on his menu—black pepper, rice wine, black bean, and the traditional sweet chili, just to name a few. The crab is broken apart and lightly steamed so it just holds together. It's cooked again in chef Yeo's killer sweet chili sauce. It's a great dish to pick through, spending some quality time cracking and working the meat out of the crab's nooks and crannies. You suck on the thick, sweet chili paste that gets all over your fingers and your face. It's probably the only time that making a huge mess is encouraged in Singapore. After I tried chili crab a couple different ways, I cleaned up with some hot towels and moved on to Yeo's newest creation: steamed shark's head.

This is a dish that Yeo claims he invented and, interestingly, it's a dish that has no meat on it at all. Singaporeans, like the rest of the world outside of our country, eat from snout to tail, using every part of the animal, because they have never lost connection with the idea that they should never waste a thing. Finances dictate it, as does culinary ideology. Yeo noticed this was not the case with shark—the heads always went to waste. He experimented with the shark's heads and ended up with a novel dish you're not going to find anywhere else.

He starts by stripping down the skin, trimming the head, and cutting out the gills. You're left with a pointy, triangular piece of bone with thick slabs of what look like pale, gelatinous tendons hanging from it. These are the connective tissues that make the jaws of the animal move up and down with such mind-boggling strength. Yeo makes lateral incisions perpendicular to the bone so that all these big flaps of cartilage protrude like fingers. He steams the shark's head in light sweet soy sauce and rice wine, which removes the pungent (and often nasty) off flavors typically present in fish heads.

After four hours of steaming, those gelatinous pieces of cartilage will melt in your mouth. Next, Yeo puts this head on a platter, drizzles it with a sturdier soy sauce, and finishes it with shaved ginger and scallion. You pull off these little bits of cartilage from the head and eat them. The texture reminds me of perfectly cooked sea cucumber, yielding a slight crunch as you sink your teeth in but melting away after just a hint of pressure. The rich, buttery flavor reminds me of bone marrow. This is one of the most unusual dishes I've ever had, but trust me, it's absolutely addictive. It sounds straight out of a sci-fi movie, but the flavor, texture, and novelty simply blew me away. It's certainly not the type of thing anyone would ever order on his own, but it's worth a try if you get the opportunity.

LITTLE INDIA

Just across the city is a completely different food experience. I toured Little India with Anita Kapoor, a local Indian woman who works as food writer and TV host. She is superbly knowledgeable and understands the food scene in Singapore, especially in her neighborhood.

The highlight for me was the Banana Leaf Apolo. This is an Indian restaurant that, though not responsible for inventing fish head curry, takes credit for making it globally famous. We sat down in this cafeteria-style eatery where you eat from banana leaves in the traditional style, ordering rice, some condiments, and bowls of curried fish heads. These aren't tiny fish heads, either, but are taken from giant red snapper with enough of the neck in place to provide ample meaty benefits in addition to little tasty treasures like the cheeks, eyes, tongue, and bits of skin.

When cooked correctly, a fish head offers so much tender and delicious meat. Frankly, I get bored with mildly flavored, everyday fillets, so every once in a while a more aggressive fish concoction just hits the spot. The spicy curried broth loaded with root vegetables, greens, onions, and tomatoes is the perfect partner to a fish head. You scoop the broth and bits of the fish head onto your rice and eat everything by hand. Never use your left hand at the table! Indian culture reserves this hand for more personal bodily functions.

A MEDICINAL MEAL

I was then back with Violet Oon, who introduced me to one of the most interesting approaches to cuisine I've ever experienced. The Imperial Herbal Restaurant in VivoCity, located on beautiful Harbourfront Walk, specializes in TCM, or Traditional Chinese Medicine. The restaurant sets out not only to nourish, but to cure whatever ails your body. The menu is chock-full of exotic ingredients: antelope horn, dried sea horse and cordyceps (a fungus), deer penis—nothing illegal, mind you. Once we arrived, we sat down with Dr. Fu, a TCM physician.

He took my pulse, examined my tongue, and checked my body by prodding and poking me all over with his fingers. He did a lot of staring at me. The consultation ended with a prescription for particular foods to cool down my body parts that had gotten overheated, warm up my parts that had gotten too cold, tone down my yang, replenish my ying . . . You aren't required to undergo the medical examination in order to eat at this remarkable eatery, but I don't understand why you wouldn't. I suppose many customers, especially locals, already have an herbalist prescribing food for their health, so they just go in and enjoy the fabulous cuisine.

THE EARLIEST CHINESE CUISINE

No trip to Singapore would be complete without eating at a Peranakan restaurant. This was the stuff I was most eager to try. Peranakans are also known as Straits Chinese, named after the Straits Settlements, a group of territories created by the British in Southeast Asia in 1826. Basically, the term refers to people in the region of Chinese descent.

Peranakan is old-school Singapore and refers to the earliest Chinese who immigrated there and intermarried with Malays, giving rise to a unique culture and cuisine. Singapore's Katong district is the place to see and experience this culture in action. The historic neighborhood houses a famous spice garden containing more than one hundred different spices that grow abundantly in Singapore.

THE BUA KELUAK NUT

It was there that I met up with a young chef named Ben Seck who comes from a family that specializes in Peranakan cooking. He introduced me to one of the strangest fruits I've ever encountered. The fruit, which grows on giant trees, contains a black nut known as a bua keluak. What's bizarre about this nut is not its flavor necessarily, but the fact that it is extremely poisonous. Detoxifying the nut is a tedious process (which I am baffled that someone ever managed to figure out in the first place), beginning with breaking the fruit open and picking out only the seeds. Next, the seeds get buried in volcanic ash for a hundred days. After the nuts are dug out of the ground, they are soaked in water for three days to wash away the ashes. After all this, each nut must be smelled before it is chopped up to ensure it hasn't gone bad. Just one bad nut will spoil an entire dish, making it toxic to consume. Once you've culled the good nuts from the bad, you can begin to work with them.

COOKED FROM MEMORY

The Seck family restaurant, True Blue Cuisine, is extremely popular in Singapore. Ben shares the cooking duties with his mother, Daisy Seah, who is arguably the most famous Peranakan chef in the country.

The restaurant is located in a restored two-story town

house, and walking through the front door is like stepping back a hundred years. What's special about the food is that the recipes are not written down. Rather, they've been passed from generation to generation. Mother and son created some of the most interesting, authentic dishes using the bua keluak nuts, including a duck soup that was just absolutely glorious with the cooked fruit. The paste from the nut smells like coffee and dark chocolate, almost like a fermented mocha with elements of burnt caramel and bitters. The paste works on the plate much like a condiment, and once you crack open the cooked nuts, you can spread the paste on anything. It enhances everything it touches, sort of like a naturally occurring Peranakan version of Vegemite.

I sampled a braised-chicken dish with fermented shrimp paste and rice. Somehow, when mixed with rice, the bua keluak lost some of that coffee and chocolate flavor and instead offered a light, citrusy finish. The nut can change flavors depending on what it's cooked with, making it the Zelig of the food world. This is a very complex and interesting ingredient, but the braised chicken was not the quintessential Peranakan dish I'd been dying to try.

THE ORIGIN OF LAKSA

No one is exactly sure how laksa earned its name. One group claims that the name stems from the Hindi-Persian word *lakhshah*, which refers to a type of noodle. Some say it's derived from the Chinese word *la-sha*, which is pronounced "lots-a" and means "spicy sand," due to the ground dried shrimp that typically goes into the soup. Another theory is that it's a Hokkien term that means "dirty," a reference to the messy appearance of the dish.

But regardless of how it came to be, "laksa" generally describes two different types of noodle soup dishes, curried laksa and assam laksa. Assam laksa is something that I've seen more often in northern Southeast Asian countries, especially in the upper half of Thailand, where the base for the dish typically is a sweet-and-sour fish soup. In Singapore, laksa is usually built around a curried coconut soup. Most of the versions are yellowish red in appearance, with dried prawns that give them a shrimpy flavor, complete with a curry gravy or soup. Thick rice noodles, known as laksa noodles, are typically used in this dish.

However, sometimes thin rice vermicelli are used, and these are known as bee hoon or mee hoon. Foodaholics will argue that one noodle or the other makes a laksa more or less of an authentic experience, but I'm not sure it's as easy as that.

I was turned on to curried laksa growing up in New York City, where we ate a lot of Thai and Indonesian food. The main ingredients of the laksas that I knew as a kid were pieces of tofu and fish, shrimp, sometimes cockles or clams, and maybe bits of julienned chicken if you were at a fancier restaurant. Many places add a nice kick by cooking chilies in the broth or by putting a spoonful of nuclear-hot sambal on top just before serving. Of course, the variety of the options—even in New York—is nothing compared to how divergently this dish is represented in Southeast Asia. Malaysians often use Vietnamese cilantro in theirs, and refer to it as daun kesum. In Penang, where I went four or five years ago, the dish is known as curried mee because of the liberal use of mee hoon noodles. Curried mee is a delicacy to the Malaysian Chinese community, especially when served with cubes of congealed pork blood. There are so many versions of laksa, it's hard to keep track. My personal favorite is Nyonya laksa, made with coconut milk. Katong laksa, a variant of Nyonya laksa, comes specifically from the Katong area of Singapore, where they cut the noodles into smaller pieces so the dish can be easily eaten with a spoon. Some people say Katong laksa is the true Singaporean national dish. I've only tried the variety with cut-up noodles two or three times, but to me, the curried laksa with long, thick noodles is king. What can I say? I'm a slurper.

MY SEARCH FOR MARY'S CORNER

I spent my entire trip to Singapore carrying around a notebook with "Mary's Corner" listed on the back. No address, just a name. Whenever we were out and about, I begged our driver to pull over if we ever glimpsed it. Near the end of the trip, we finally found this humble little restaurant. As is often the case with any good eater, sometimes you have to take hostages, and at times my crew suffers the slings and arrows of being pulled like little bits of flotsam and jetsam in a storm all over cities in search of certain types of food. This was no exception. I made everyone have some.

Mary's is situated in the Nan Sin Eating House on East Coast Road, with two or three outdoor tables. Orders are placed at a window on the street that fronts the postage-stamp-size kitchen. You get your bowl, sit at one of the tables, slurp down your soup, and move along. At peak hours, the line stretches around the corner, with most people opting to have their laksa to go.

On our visit, I took a moment to peer into the kitchen, where I could see down a narrow space that reached about forty feet back into the rear storage rooms, all the way through to another business in the next building. This interior hall led to the prep area, where I spied Mary presiding over a giant vat—almost like a garbage can—of boiling soup. The noodles are cooked separately and the old woman puts them into a bowl; ladles the liquid gold over the noodles; scatters poached shrimp, bean sprouts, cilantro, sambal, and bits of tofu on top; and hands you a steaming-hot bowl of goodness.

While this might sound like a simple operation, the guys she's got making noodles to order would beg to differ. And when I say made to order, I mean made from scratch, hand-rolled in multiple portions, batches-to-order. That to me is one of the hallmarks of a great laksa. Are you pounding your own paste for your soup? Are you making your own noodles? At Mary's, they cook thirty or forty portions of handmade noodles at a time. There's not a knife; there's not a cutter or machine. Instead, they use that old Chinese repetitive knead-and-fold methodology.

After repeating this process for about eight minutes, the noodle maker basically raises the tube of dough up over his head and slams it on the table, where it explodes into a thousand strands of pasta. It's one of the most glorious techniques I've ever seen.

Mary's laksa was impressive. Sure, it had the sandy,

ground-up dried shrimp. It had the rich coconut milk I adore. It had the traditional, thick white laksa noodles. And, yes, it had a curry flavor. But what really put this soup in a league of its own was the fact that it wasn't made with a fish soup base, but instead was created with a strong, rich, briny, and crustaceously awesome shrimp soup. When that base was cooked with the coconut milk, you ended up with one of the best spicy Asian shellfish bisques that I've ever encountered. Sprinkle that soup with some ground nuts, the bean sprouts, the cilantro, a lime wedge, sambal (chile sauce), the blan-chan (dried shrimp paste), and you have a dangerously sweet, sour, salty seafood noodle explosion on your hands.

I realize I throw around superlatives a little too much, and I'm always warning myself not to say things like "it was the best bowl of soup I had ever had," but boy, I'm drooling just sitting here writing this. I can taste that shrimpy good-ness and can almost feel the sweat popping out between my eyebrows, which lets you know the soup is perfectly and in-tensely infused with chilies. You can't stop eating it. I admit, I might be romanticizing this soup a little because the near-est bowl is three thousand miles away. Or maybe it's the fact that I may never have the opportunity to devour it again. But having said that, I still insist that the simplicity of the dish, the freshness of the noodles, and the immediacy of the cooking preparation made this my ideal bowl of laksa.

Simple Foods:
Noodle Houses of Guangzhou

My love of Chinese food borders on obsession. For the record, this Chinese food I speak of is not a plate of indistinguishable fried hunks of meat, tossed in a wok and coated with a sticky cornstarch-based sauce. That's an American take on Chinese food, something you often find at food courts. I occasionally indulge in this all-you-can-eat buffet-style Chinese food, but trust me, real Chinese food it isn't. You don't need to travel to the People's Republic to find authentic Chinese food. I've experienced some of the most authentic Sichuan food in St. Paul, Minnesota. All that is required is access to ingredients and a good skill set in the kitchen. Honesty and authenticity don't have a lot to do with location, although location often helps.

Few people in the world have a more passionate relationship with food than the Chinese. Due to large-scale immigration from the southern province of Guangdong to the rest of the world, Cantonese cuisine is by far China's best known. Cantonese cuisine originated in Canton, which is now called Guangzhou. With its fertile soil, perfect for growing all kinds of vegetables and raising healthy animals, as well as proximity to rivers, lakes, and oceans, Guangzhou puts every ingredient you could possibly want within reach. And if the people there can reach it, they'll eat it. As an old Cantonese adage says, if it walks, swims, crawls, or flies with its back to heaven, it must be edible. Cantonese live by those words. They will eat anything and everything. It's not that they are obsessed with exotic foods; it's just that if it tastes good, they'll eat it.

THE GUANGZHOU RESTAURANT

The simply named Guangzhou Restaurant is the city's most popular. Founded in 1935, it is the oldest operating restaurant in Guangzhou. You'd think that, in a country as storied and steeped in history, there would be some form of eatery still in operation predating 1935 in this eater's city, but there isn't. Its original name was Xi Nan Restaurant, but when the People's Republic was established, the name was changed to the nondescript, egalitarian one the restaurant has today. Despite the name change, the food remained the same. In fact, many dishes are just as famous today as they were at the restaurant's inception, most notably the dim sum. Guangzhou Restaurant is located at the busy merging of

Wenchang Nan Road and Shangxiajiu Street, one of the most famous intersections in the Li Wan district. Over the years, it's expanded from just a restaurant on the first floor to a catering and banquet service, housed on the second and third floors. They feed as many as ten thousand people a day at the original location, and run affiliated branches from Hong Kong to Los Angeles. I'm sure you can eat a fine meal at any of their outposts, but you can't beat a meal at the original.

The main dining room is all about classic Cantonese food served in a beautiful classic setting. An antique stained-glass window from the Ching dynasty hangs in the main dining room, with a giant *rongshu* (banyan tree) spreading overhead. The restaurant is composed of numerous courtyards and rooms connected by arcade corridors. The waitstaff, dressed in traditional Ching dynasty servant uniforms, gives the dining experience the air of taking a step back in time. Add the fact that they've mastered Cantonese cuisine, and you have a hard time convincing me that if you could eat only one meal in Guangzhou, it shouldn't be here.

SIGNATURE DISHES

The Guangzhou Restaurant is known for its dim sum, which was decent but not half as good as that found at other places I'd visited in China or Taiwan. But if you're looking for traditional Cantonese cuisine, look no further. Cantonese cuisine offers a rather mild flavor profile and consists of contrasting elements. When it comes to flavors and styles, you're not going to get a one-note Charlie, and when dinner is all said and done, often you've enjoyed a steamed dish, a cold dish, a boiled dish, a spicy dish, and a double-fried dish. I had duck soup with Chinese watermelon, and a bowl of creamy northeast Chinese peanuts simmered with the black skins still intact. Interestingly, they use a lot of milk skin in dishes, which struck me as odd. Milk skin is made by boiling fresh milk until a fine layer of skin is formed. After the milk cools, the liquid separates from the skin, making a congealed, fatty, egg-white-like substance that offers a textural counterpoint to most other dishes. While I didn't care for the milk skin in savory dishes, I really liked it served as a dessert. Their double-skin milk, braised with sugar forming yet another layer of skin, is sweeter still. Caramel heaven.

The dish that sticks out most in my mind is their Wenchang chicken. Such special care goes into creating this impeccable dish that it's difficult not to swoon over it. These chickens are to China what Wagyu beef is to Japan. The chickens are tenderly cared for, raised in coops high off the ground and fed a specific diet of coconut, peanut cakes, and banyan seeds. As a result, the meat becomes fatty, with the skin turning yellow and very brittle when cooked. Guangzhou Restaurant's version is cooked twice, steamed at first, then deboned, plated, and steamed again to heat it back up. It's finished with a light, aromatic sauce of aged soy sauce and faintly salty and briny abalone. It's even said that a Cantonese meal without traditional Wenchang chicken is really no meal at all.

But my meal at Guangzhou Restaurant that day was just the beginning; I needed to see for myself one of Cantonese food's crowning glories, the noodle house. Noodles are the primary component of many Chinese dishes. At one time, all noodles were made by hand in homes and restaurants. Modern machinery has since taken over that process, but fortunately for me, the art of hand-pulled noodles is still practiced at the Jiu Mao Jiu Noodle Restaurant. This place is all about the noodles, and they make dozens of varieties from scratch.

Aside from great noodle dishes, China is also known for its odd translations of the English language on signs, menus, T-shirts, and more. Due to the recent massive tourism push, mainly for the Beijing 2008 Olympic Games and the Expo 2010 Shanghai China (the most expensive world's fair of all time), the Chinese government has been determined to fix hundreds of thousands of erroneous signs. The Chinese do have a point—signs are supposed to be helpful, not confusing. However, Chinglish lovers like myself hope they leave many of the signs alone—they're hysterical. Here are some of my favorites:

~What the sign means: Please don't cross the street.
What the sign actually says: The front not opened section road, no passing!

~What the sign means: Watch your step.
What the sign actually says: Don't fall down!

~What the sign means: During thunderstorms, cell phone use is prohibited.
What the sign actually says: Speaking cellphone is strictly prohibited when thunderstorm.

~What the sign means: Cherish cultural relics—no graffiti, please.
What the sign actually says: Cherish the cultural relic—please don't scribble.

~What the sign means: Please don't flush toilet paper.
What the sign actually says: Please do not put any paper in the toilet. You will see DISASTER!

> ~What the sign means: Please stay off the grass.
> What the sign actually says: Do not disturb—tiny grass is dreaming!
>
> ~What the sign means: I'm really not sure. . . .
> What the sign actually says: Please keep the toilet clean and don't feed the toilet.

Jiu Mao Jiu, also dubbed the **Noodle King,** takes its noodles seriously. The noodles are made by a trained cook who spends years perfecting the art form. The noodle paste or dough is made by hand in massive work bowls, and through a series of stretching and pulling maneuvers the dough becomes pliable, then gets rolled back up into a ball. The ball is rolled out into a fat tube until it's about four feet long, then the ends are joined, the dough is twisted, and the process is repeated a hundred times. Every time the ends are joined, the middle of the long tube of dough is swung so it twists around itself, then gets stretched again.

Then, on a cutting board, the noodle maker begins pulling the dough with his arms outstretched, folding the thick strings of dough in two with fewer refolds in between stretches. He pulls again and again and again until the strings of dough become longer and more numerous, thinner and thinner, finally turning the mass into very fine noodles. It's an art form requiring extreme dexterity.

Stir-fried dishes are cooked in a closed kitchen here, but all the noodle stuff is done in the **open.** It's a slightly less cheesy Benihana teppanyaki show that concludes with food that actually tastes really good. You can also watch as these experts turn balls of dough into delicate noodle chips right before your eyes. They take a sharp tool that looks like a four-inch spackling knife, then strike the ball of dough sitting in their opposite hand outward, away from their body, sending little chips of raw noodle dough into a giant wok of boiling water six feet away. These fat, thick, doughy globs get cooked, then sauced. The process reminded me of flipping playing cards into a hat, except that these guys had great aim.

 During the Sung dynasty (AD 960–1280), noodle shops were very popular in the cities, and they remained open all night. Think of them as the ancient Chinese version of your favorite pizza shop.

Jiu Mao Jiu also creates noodles literally as thin as silk thread, formed through a process where they keep folding and refolding the noodles, weaving and reweaving the dough to a point where they dramatically smash it on a table, exploding the dough into hundreds of thin noodles. It's like solving a Rubik's Cube—I have seen it done, but I can't explain it.

The Chinese equate long noodles with a **long life,** and therefore have created a method that turns dough into spaghetti-thin strands of single noodles that stretch hundreds of feet long. In fact, the only limit to a noodle's length is how much dough is available. These long single noodles are the basis of big noodle bowls here at Jiu Mao Jiu.

In a quality restaurant like Jiu Mao Jiu, it's one noodle, just piled in there, coiled on top of itself. This is executed by weaving the noodle by hand, then spooling the dough from the noodle maker's hand into a giant bowl of water. The strand of dough is quickly pulled from the bowl and tossed into a cooking pot. The dough is cut only when the right

The Chinese, Arabs, and Italians all claim to be the first noodle makers; the Chinese documented noodles' existence in writing between AD 25 and AD 220. In 2005, a four-thousand-year-old bowl of noodles was found underneath ten feet of sediment at Lajia, in northwestern China. This is the earliest example ever found of one of the world's most popular foods. Scientists now call Asia—not Italy—the birthplace of the noodle.

proportion of noodle has been achieved. Order up a bowl of minced pork with black bean sauce, and out comes a big soup bowl filled with enough noodle to feed two or three people, the whole dish swimming in porky, beany goodness.

MY FAVORITE DISH

Noodles, of course, need accompaniments, and the kitchen staff were just as skillful at dressing up a noodle as they were in constructing it. I fell in love with a dish made with cat's ear noodles. These tiny noodles start life as flat dough triangles, no larger than a half-inch wide at the base, and are pinched together in such a way that when dropped in the water, they swell dramatically, softening the angular edges. The result: curled shapes that looked just like teeny cat's ears. When these noodles were cooked in a wok with a light vinegar sauce, bits of minced meat, and scallion, the first bite exploded with flavor. The tart edge to the sauce just made the dish seem lighter, allowing you to eat a lot more than is probably advisable.

I was amazed by a dish called "kow-low-low," which translates as "standing shoulder to shoulder." This dish is made with thick, sturdy, hollow noodles lined up to symbolize strength and unity. The noodles are put into a dim sum steamer standing on end, packed tightly so they don't topple over on their sides (then they would be cheek by jowl, a slightly less Maoist food metaphor than shoulder to shoulder). A plate of these conjoined noodles arrives at the table with a rich, earthy oyster sauce, sautéed minced pork, ginger, and aged fermented black beans spooned over the top. Using your chopsticks, you pull apart these starchy tubes that have been steamed together and are dripping with the meaty, rich, salty-sweet sauce.

In addition to phenomenal noodles, I sampled stir-fry dishes at Jiu Mao Jiu that remain some of my all-time favorites. I'll never forget the twice-cooked pork with garlic sauce, which had the wok dragon's breath still on it. That's the kind of charry, smoky flavor and aroma you'll get only from food that's been properly scorched in the hottest of woks and then whisked to your table so fast that you can still taste the wok's heat with your first bite.

So with all apologies to those of Italian heritage reading this book, as amazing as many of the pasta dishes that I've eaten in Italy are, and no matter how many Italian restaurants around the world I have visited and fallen in love with, I'd have to say without a doubt that the best noodle experience I've ever had has been at Jiu Mao Jiu in Guangzhou.

Fish Heaven:
Finding Perfection
in a Ginza Basement

Although it has yet to achieve the everyday normalcy hot dogs and doughnuts have in this country, sushi is perhaps the most popular food in the United States, possibly in the world. Over the last five years, hundreds of millions of Russian and Chinese middle-class consumers came online, joining the legions of global sushi nuts. Demand increased so drastically that the prices high-quality fish were able to garner at wholesale fish markets around the world hiccupped forward almost overnight, responding to and then resulting in a sea change in demand.

The Japanese have long enjoyed a food made by salting and drying small lake fish, then packing it in cooked rice, leaving it to ferment in barrels. The pickled fish product plucked from those barrels over a year later was called funa-zushi. The Japanese loved it, and funa-zushi became cheap, convenient peasant fare consumed both for pleasure and out of necessity.

During the Edo period, which began in the early seventeenth century, gambling became very popular. People would sit in small taverns and mark their cards, dice, or playing tiles with rice that had stuck to the pickled fish, or with grains from their rice bowls. Enterprising tavern owners began offering a snack alternative. They kept the funa-zushi and the rice, but they wrapped the two together in nori, edible paper made of seaweed. Thus began the world's obsession with sushi—but thankfully, today the fish is a lot fresher.

I remember when Japanese food was essentially a handful of little yakitori-style restaurants in Manhattan. I was probably eleven or twelve when my friends, the Wakabayashi family, began taking me to Tenryu on a weekly basis. Invariably, one of our appetizers was a large platter of assorted sashimi and sushi. Around the same time, I began accompanying my dad to lunches and dinners at the old (and long-since-closed) Edo in the West Forties. Like most sushi newcomers, I first fell in love with tekka maki, those small chunks of tuna rolled in rice and nori. I eventually graduated to eel, freshwater and saltwater; *hamachi* (young yellowtail); then to geoduck, known in Japan as *mirugai*. This gigantic saltwater clam soon became my favorite.

The first time I tried *uni*, or sea urchin, was at Hatsuhana. The liver-y and softly textured creamy roe of the sea urchin isn't for everyone, but I adored its one-of-a-kind saline and minerally flavor profile. This was the place to eat sushi and sashimi in the late 1970s. I would sit mesmerized for hours as I watched the brigade of sushi chefs with long, thin blades turning four-inch chunks of cucumber into paper-thin sheets. They would make their thin cucumber paper, roll it around in thin warm slices of *unagi* (freshwater eel), then slice it thin, creating little eel and cucumber pinwheels, one of their first signature dishes.

TO THE MARKET

I love sushi and sashimi, and I've eaten some great fish in my day. Still, to my mind, one of the great experiences in my food life was getting up at oh-dark-thirty and heading over to Tsukiji Market in Tokyo to watch the fresh- and frozen-tuna auctions. Participants still dress up in the ancient uniforms, march into the auction room, and bid away for some of the most beautiful fish you've ever seen in your life. I've had the honor of escorting three-hundred-pound fish from the market floor at four in the morning to a dealer's booth. This wholesaler cut up the fish, dispensing pieces to sushi restaurants around the greater Tokyo metro area who had placed orders with him that day. I watched the cutters take six-foot-long samurai swords and divide the fish into panels, separating the *chutoro* from the *otoro* and the *toro* from the *guro*. He weighed the different cuts of tuna, wrapped the order up, and sent it on its way.

I've learned more about tuna from spending a few days at Tsukiji Market than I ever did eating and working in restaurants. I've prowled the market extensively, hopping booth to booth, tasting tuna brought in from different parts of the world. I've had wholesalers lead me by the hand to the carcass of mammoth bluefin and yellowfin tuna, where they'd run a spoon along certain bones or along the spinal cord, collecting scrapings of particularly fatty or noteworthy bites to educate me on what to look for in terms of fat content, flavor, and texture.

I've eaten some of the most world-renowned sushi. I've been lucky enough to dine at Nobu Matsuhisa's restaurants many times. I've probably visited eight or nine of them globally, often getting fed by the master himself. I didn't think anything could top having Nobu Matsuhisa himself prepare *uni*, raw scallop, a selection of *toro*, and more for me, as he stood behind the sushi bar at his restaurant one night in Los Angeles. This was the thrill of a lifetime—until I got a chance to eat with him in the kitchen of his Tokyo restaurant a year later. If you've never eaten poached octopus eggs cooked in dashi (Japanese soup stock) and mirin, accompanied by some fresh fried frog, I can tell you it's imperative to do so one day.

And speaking of frog, not in my wildest dreams did I ever consider eating frog sashimi. They serve it in Japan at a little *getemono* bar called the Asadachi. Tokyo's *getemono* bars are notorious for serving food-forward, psyche-challenging dishes, so if you have a craving for a grilled lizard, that's where you go. Businessmen flock to these little restaurants to eat for sport, usually as a way to celebrate the closing of an auspicious business deal. Eating frog sashimi involved more audience participation than I'd anticipated. I actually selected my live frog from a basket. The chef then took a penknife and ripped its skin off. He served me paper-thin slices of the frog's flesh with a bit of soy and lemon sauce for dipping, along with a separate bowl for the still-beating frog's heart.

I am not in the business of animal cruelty, and the debate can rage on for decades about whether or not a lobster has "feelings," but there are many cases (oysters, clams, to name a few) where lively freshness is imperative when dining, and, frankly, in most cases I am very content being ensconced firmly at the top of the food chain. I would also say

I love sushi. A lot of people think sushi is just about raw slices of fish, but that's not always the case. You can order maki—rolls of sweet, sticky rice topped with fish or vegetables and wrapped up in nori, or seaweed (kind of like a mini burrito). Nigiri is sliced pieces of fish placed atop a firm pad of rice. Sashimi is the sliced raw fish served straight up. Navigating a sushi menu can be a daunting task, with lots of unfamiliar words on the menu. For those of you with sushi anxiety, I've put together a list of my favorite items, in no particular order.

~**Tekka maki.** This was the first type of sushi I fell in love with, and my five-year-old son loves it as well! It's simple: raw tuna and rice rolled in nori. Dunk each cylindrical piece in a dish of soy sauce and eat the whole thing in one big bite.

~*Unagi.* If the idea of eating raw fish creeps you out, start off with barbecued *unagi,* or freshwater eel. Sure, eel sounds pretty weird, too, but it's fully cooked and covered in a sweet and savory Japanese sauce.

~*Maguro.* This slice of raw bluefin tuna is a deep red, and it is a definite crowd pleaser. A high-quality piece of *maguro* will have a mild flavor and a meaty texture.

~**Hamachi.** A good piece of *hamachi,* or young yellowtail, will melt in your mouth. One bite of *hamachi,* flavorful and buttery, will turn you into a fan for life.

~**Tobiko.** These tiny little spheres are fish eggs, the roe of flying fish. They sometimes are sprinkled over rolls for a slight crunch, but I prefer to order them off the nigiri menu. Hundreds of these eggs are placed on a pad of rice, then wrapped in nori. They pop in your mouth, kind of like bubble wrap. It's really fun to eat.

~**Hikarimono.** Silver-skinned fish sliced for serving, with the silver skin left on. You actually eat the silvery fish scales.

~**Mirugai.** Raw geoduck, a huge clam that resembles a certain male appendage (wink wink). It's sweet and slightly crunchy— much like a cucumber.

~**Amaebi.** Sure, eating sweet shrimp, served raw, is pretty good. However, most sushi bars will serve you the shrimp heads, deep-fried, as an accompaniment. They're absolutely delicious. For the record, you're supposed to eat the eyes, antennae, shell, and all.

~**Uni.** The gonad of a sea urchin, this is one of those foods that people either love or hate. *Uni* are gold in color, and are typically sweet and creamy.

~**Fugu.** The innards and blood of this fish, also known as blowfish or puffer fish, contain a deadly poison. Only licensed chefs are allowed to prepare the fish. *Fugu* tastes fine, but the real attraction is the danger associated with this meal. A master sushi chef will serve every edible part of the *fugu*—not just the flesh but the liver, intestines, and skin.

that many of the more extreme examples of my dining on live animals falls into the experiential category and not into the everyday-habit category.

There certainly is a lot of culinary magic going on in

Japan, and not just with the restaurants. Good Japanese cooks—and I've had the pleasure of working with many in my life—are brilliant replicators. So precise, with impeccable knife skills. Their diligence, discipline, and powers of concentration are far beyond the average Western cook's. Give them a classic French or Italian dish and within a day they can nail it every time. The great French and Italian restaurants in Tokyo are hindered only by availability of ingredients, which in the age of the airplane does not limit them much at all. But the last time I was in Tokyo, I had the opportunity to have a meal—alone, in an empty restaurant in between lunch and dinner—that stands to this day as the greatest single sushi experience I've ever had.

THE BEST OF THE BEST

Sushi Mizutani is a teeny restaurant in the basement of the Ginza Seiwa Silver Building, right around the corner from the Shimbashi Station. Open six days a week, serving lunch and dinner Monday through Friday, this gem is the best sushi restaurant in Tokyo.

Behind the counter is a space that is only big enough for one person to walk through at a time, and there is only one chef here, so no need for more room. A table for two, tucked away in the corner across from the sushi bar, may be used at dinnertime, but only when Chef Mizutani deems it fitting to seat someone there. He loves to dole food out himself, lavishing stories on his patrons, allowing them a front-and-center seat to what may be the greatest set of sushi skills operating in the world. Mizutani is the man. Every bite of food in this restaurant passes through his hands at some point.

The real magic happens before the restaurant even opens, when Mizutani himself, along with his assistant, prowls the markets, collecting the best product available in the city—and with almost fifty years of cooking under his belt, he knows what he's looking for. He's a neat and tidy little man, very thin, with a big, round face and an easy smile. His giant round glasses emphasize the curving features of his face. He's probably approaching seventy if he's not already there, but he has the energy of a man half his age.

His restaurant is spare and without pretension. You actually go down into the building's basement, where you'll find a nondescript sliding screen door. You knock and enter. It's one of the more hidden-away restaurants that I've ever experienced, especially for one of this caliber, but Mizutani doesn't want it any other way.

He's been there for years now, doing what he does like no other: simply providing people with the best. The best-quality fish and shellfish, the best aged soy sauce, the best shari (vinegared rice).

Every ingredient has a special provenance. His rice, for example, comes from a handful of growers at a very special farm a couple hundred miles south of his Tokyo eatery. The vinegar he seasons his rice with is made in a renowned prefecture in northern Japan. His dishes have few ingredients, but each one is comprised of the highest quality foodstuffs available.

I think the food world has come full circle in many ways.

It used to be that all food was served on platters with everyone sharing family-style. Over the course of the next couple of hundred years, from the sixteenth to the eighteenth century, taverns came into vogue; by the end of the eighteenth century, restaurants were popular. Real restaurant culture developed in Europe in the early nineteenth century, but taverns—simple places to enjoy a meal—well, these eateries have existed for centuries. Serving individual foods plated in single-portion is a relatively modern convention that began in the 1700s and developed with the rise of a true middle class—average, everyday folks who began to accumulate some disposable income. Give a man an extra dollar and chances are he will spend it on food.

THE FOOD VS. THE CHEF

For hundreds of years, it was restaurants themselves—not the food or chef—that were famous. Of course, many chefs garnered fame for inventing certain dishes at certain restaurants, especially in America. Chefs of New York's Delmonico's restaurant in the nineteenth century were justifiably famous, not necessarily by name or face, but by reputation. And it didn't matter who was cooking—you always knew someone good was there, much as it is at Commander's Palace in New Orleans today. This has been home to some of the greatest chefs working in the South. You knew every time you went there, year in and year out, that it was going to be good.

For the past few decades, restaurants have been all about the chef. While some of today's chefs have achieved rock star status (hello, Wolfgang Puck), the quality of the ingredients is just as important as the person cooking them.

You go to many restaurants not just to see what a certain chef can do with a given menu or oeuvre, but to eat food made with ingredients available nowhere else. Sometimes the chef and his ingredients are synonymous. Today, it's all about ingredient worship, and I think sushi bars are the most obvious places to witness that development.

IT'S ALL ABOUT THE INGREDIENTS

When it comes to ingredients, Japan's respect for food matches Italy's passion and simplicity. Like Japanese cuisine, Italian food at its essence is extremely simple, extremely seasonal, and not overly complex or clichéd. But the Japanese are indeed special. I think it's the only culture in the world where a single pickled plum served on a giant plate gets the kind of oohs and aahs that elsewhere are reserved for more ambitious culinary pyrotechnics.

In Japan, "simple" really works in a way that it doesn't elsewhere. It's pretentious when I see that type of cooking in other restaurants; they are just imitators and replicators, as opposed to true disciples. When you're in a Japanese restaurant where a chef is actually making complex philosophical decisions about what to put on a plate, it can get really impressive. Japanese chefs would never serve that plum at its peak of ripeness just sitting naked on a dish; they would feel obligated to cook or prepare it in some way, even subtly. I mean, that's why you go to a restaurant, right? If you wanted to eat the perfect raw plum, you'd go see a farmer; you wouldn't go see a chef. But—and it's a big but—if anyone serves food in a more naked or exposed or simple manner than the Japanese do, I haven't seen it.

Great Japanese chefs do just enough to those special items to heighten the eating experience without killing the ingredient. An ingredient captured at its peak moment of

---

Sushi Etiquette

~Though you'll receive chopsticks at most sushi places, it's A-OK to eat sushi with your bare hands—even in fancy restaurants.

~Many people like to dip their sushi into a dish of soy sauce. While that's fine, keep in mind that, traditionally, sushi is dipped fish—not rice—side down.

~Don't rub your chopsticks together. It's a sign to the waitstaff that you think the restaurant is cheap.

~Eat nigiri-style sushi in one bite. This is not always easy (or possible) in North America, where some *sushi-ya* make huge pieces, so just use your best judgment.

~Never leave your chopsticks sticking up in your rice. This is a bad omen, as it resembles symbolism used in Japanese funerals.

~The pickled ginger slices are intended to cleanse your palate in between bites—kind of like a moist towelette for the mouth. They are not meant to be eaten in the same bite as a piece of sushi.

~Watch out for the green stuff. Wasabi, or the small green mound on a sushi platter, can be delicious or a disaster. Wasabi is Japanese horseradish, and a dab is all you will probably need. Taking too much at once is a rookie mistake—one that will be rewarded with an intense burning sensation in the nose accompanied by teary eyes. Symptoms dissipate quickly, but knowing how much is too much will stick with you for life.

---

texture and flavor may not need much tweaking, which is why Mizutani's less-is-more approach works.

Mizutani himself greeted me at the door while his wife and assistant tidied up the kitchen—it's still a restaurant, after all. He invited me to sit at the sushi bar and asked me for my order. Who would better know what to order than Mizutani himself? I opted for an *omakase*-style meal, where you let the chef take the reins and you pray for the best.

Of course, I had nothing to worry about here. Mizutani serves only the best. Japan grows great rice, and Mizutani has been getting his from the same family for years. All their rice is hand-planted, tended, and harvested in small batches. The care with which Mizutani prepares the rice is astounding. He washes and dries it, then gently cooks and seasons it with his specially formulated vinegars to give it a faint sweetness. This special care extends to the way he cuts and stores his fish, and the way he handles individual pieces of fish, especially ones with a high fat content—like certain cuts of tuna—not allowing the warmth of his hand to change the texture of the fish. Rice. Fish. Plate. Simple, but not easy.

I watched as he handled the *saba*, or mackerel. He cups the fish in his hand, keeping his palm in contact with the rice for different lengths of time depending on the fish itself, transforming the flavor for the better, making it less fishy and less oily, as the warmth of the rice and his hand actually draws some of that oil from the fish into the rice itself. In a sense, he cooks with his hands.

It's not that Mizutani serves the most unusual fish. My meal ran the full gamut of traditional seafood, such as *akagai*, *mirugai*, and *hokkigai*. However, superior freshness, presentation, and symphony of texture exalted this meal to a new level. I ate several different types of *hirame*, or flounder. The dorsal fin was one of the most fabulous textures of any sushi I've ever eaten: crisp and corrugated, sweet and briny. The monkfish liver was kissed with sake and mirin, warmed ever so slightly. Mizutani followed up with paper-thin slices of abalone draped over rice sushi-style, *chutoro* (which is the meaty and fatty cut of bluefin tuna taken from the belly), incredibly fatty *otoro* as well, along with *maguro*.

The squid was so fresh and delicate, cut with a dazzling sort of diamond cutter's expertise. Millions of little knife marks ran across the flesh in a crosshatch pattern, allowing the fish to simply disappear on your tongue. I had two types of eel, freshwater and saltwater, braised in a soy, sugar, and mirin sauce reduced to a syrup. The fish is cooled and cut to order, sauced and thrown under a broiler to char the edges, then draped over small balls of rice.

Mizutani served the best *uni* that I've ever eaten in my life. The shad that I had, a small bony fish that is called *kohada*, is usually a very pedestrian sort of fish in America, but in the hands of Mizutani, it was absolutely insane. His knife work is amazing, and he left little bits of skin on the shad but cut away other little pieces of the skin so it, too, disappeared in the mouth. I had *aji*, a Spanish horse mackerel minced as a little sashimi course, that was ethereal. These offerings are normally fishy even in the best of eateries; here they aren't. And his cooking skill is amazing.

Everybody raves about his tamago. This egg dish is made in a square or oblong pan; it is cooked in thin sheets and folded on itself, then pressed into a block. It is typically sweetened, and it makes a great last bite in a sushi meal. Mizutani's tamago was creamy and textured in a way that reminded me of ripe peaches.

MASTERING FOOD

I'm a big student of art history. In that field, we always talk about the space that sculptures occupy, but more important, we also talk about the negative space where something isn't. Often, less is more. It's the greatest discipline challenge for chefs. I love young, bold, brash chefs. I love to eat their food. Their experimentation is awesome, but often there is one ingredient too many on the plate. A bold, brash chef who's been around the block a few times yet still harbors that energy and curiosity in the kitchen relies less on gimmicks and needs fewer ingredients. Ingredients, pyrotechnics, and architecture in the kitchen are a great way to cover up lack of skill. Serving a single piece of fish placed on a small mound of vinegar rice is naked cooking. You're on a tightrope without a net. This simplicity and this greatness come only from those who understand that all good cooking stems from good shopping.

But Mizutani is more than a shopper. He's disciplined enough to buy only foods at their peak of flavor. He knows the best way to handle and prepare a fish. He is a master, and that is what he loves the most. This passion translates to patrons. A great restaurateur knows great food doesn't end in the kitchen. It ends on the table.

Nature's Candy: The Achachairu

When it comes to global cuisine, I've tasted it all: whole roast sparrows in Vietnam, stinky tofu in Taiwan, a glass of warm steer's blood in Uganda. As the Cantonese say, anything that walks, swims, crawls, or flies with its back to heaven is edible. I can tell you firsthand, the Cantonese are on to something. Considering the range of crazy foods I've eaten in my life, it might shock you to know that my most memorable food experiences involve fruits. This certainly shocked the heck out of me. I never would have guessed that my most thrilling food moments would come in the form of a juicy bite of fruit. Whether it's rare and exotic or ridiculously plentiful, you can't beat fruit grown in the ideal environment, picked at the right time. It's nature's candy.

MY FIRST EXOTIC FOOD EXPERIENCE

Mangosteens were the first exotic fruit that opened up a world of new ideas for me. Often referred to as the queen of all fruits, mangosteens are universally well regarded for their sweet, succulent flavor. It's like eating a sorcerer's blend of honey blossoms and wildflowers ingeniously mated with the sweetest melon. These small, round fruits have a sturdy green stem and a firm, purple, husky exterior. Place the fruit between your hands, making sure to not crush the delicious center to smithereens, press your palms together, and crack the spongy, fibrous shell. Inside, you'll uncover eight or nine misshapen segments around a central core. It's not entirely unlike a snow-white mandarin orange. Sweet and juicy, and once you take a bite, you can't stop. What makes mangosteens extra special is their relative scarcity around the world outside of their growing zones. The small mites that live inside their thick skins make these fruits next to impossible to transport, and attempts to cultivate the fruit in places with similar climates, like Hawaii, California, and Florida, have failed miserably. While I wish we all had better access to this incredible fruit, there is something to be said for being able to eat it only while in a specific area of the world. Why? Because when it comes to food, I believe in eating with the seasons. Can't really enjoy a summer tomato unless you eat beans and stew all winter long. And in the age of the jet plane and in a time when all our lives are built around instant gratification, it's nice to have something to look forward to when you travel.

MARULA

One of the most interesting fruits I've ever tasted hails from Botswana's Kalahari Desert. The marula trees drop yellow, golf-ball-size fruit, which sun-ripen (rot, actually) on the ground. Marula fruit, with an extremely tart frontal assault and a sweet finish, is not only a bushman favorite but is popular with the kudu and baboons as well. Unearthing the small bit of fruit is an involved process. You bite through the rind, remove the cap, and then squeeze the fruit from the end. The fruit pops into your mouth like an oversize lychee. Suck out the sweet-sour flesh and spit out the big seed—but don't throw it away. When roasted and dried, this seed can be cracked open and eaten. For thousands of years, marula nuts have been one of the five primary staples of the bushman's diet. I savor the simple pleasure of walking through the desert, ten marula fruits in hand, snacking on them as juice streams down my face and hands. SweeTarts never tasted so good.

As I ate my first marula fruit, it brought me right back to Santa Cruz, Bolivia, where I first tasted my favorite fruit of all time. For twenty years, I measured everything against the mangosteen. Tree-ripened apricots from the mountains a day's ride outside Marrakesh, Morocco, placed a close second. That is, until both were trumped by the achachairu.

THE BEST FRESH FRUIT STANDS

Compared to the stark, cold, and brown lunar landscapes that sweep most of Bolivia, Santa Cruz is a lush tropical paradise. Serving as the country's gateway to the Amazon, this area teems with amazing produce and wildlife. The crew and I headed to Yacapani, an even smaller town in the area that boasts a restaurant whose reputation for serving some of the world's best fish and roasted armadillo reached me all the way back in America. Some people love licorice, beef jerky, or ice cream on road trips, but to me nothing accompanies a long, dusty car ride quite like fresh fruit. I'm always on the lookout for roadside fruit stands. Taking out your penknife and cutting into a fresh papaya, melon, or bunch of bananas on a road trip is my idea of heaven.

The first fruit stand we encountered outside of Santa Cruz was filled with watermelon, avocado, and baskets of a strange citrus fruit. However, the stand looked a little down on its luck. There is nothing more disappointing than fruit that is not up to snuff—I'd rather eat my Puma sneakers than a mealy pear or a flavorless melon. My driver assured me there would be more stands along the road. Sure enough, we pulled over at a gem of a place ten minutes later. Mesh baskets hung from the wooden edge of the lean-to that protected the fruit from the hot noonday sun. At first glance, the baskets looked to be full of small lemons or limes. Upon closer inspection, I realized I'd never seen anything like this fruit: pale orange in color, some almost flaming red, and figlike in appearance, with a harder, leathery skin, much like the marula fruit.

"It's called an 'achachairu,'" the vendor explained. "It's a fruit." Sounded more like a sneeze to me, but I purchased a small bag anyhow. I was smitten.

Attacking a foreign fruit can be complicated business. It's

crucial for the neophyte to ask how to eat it. Imagine diving into a coconut, pineapple, or banana without any guidance. Do you bite into it like an apple from the orchard? Peel it like an orange? Like the marula fruit, lychee, and rambutan, the achachairu must be opened in order to access the fruit. But instead of a tidbit of white flesh surrounding a large nut, it's the exact opposite. The skin is rather thin compared to its cousins', so slipping the fruit out is a much easier endeavor. Inside, you will find a huge bite of the most delicious floral, sour symphony of flavors, which explodes into your mouth.

Advice to exotic-fruit lovers: Never ever, ever, ever buy a small piece of fruit for a couple of pennies and get back in

---

The Seven Weirdest Fruits in the World

~Frankenfruits. The Grapple (grape + apple), Pluot (plum + apricot), and Aprium (apricot + plum) all weird me out. These—or varieties of them—are actually corporately branded fruits sitting at your local supermarket. I find it mind-boggling that there are actually scientists devoting their brainpower to making frankenfruits. Why fuss with something Mother Nature was already doing perfectly fine on her own?

~Durian. My archnemesis, this is one of the most revolting foods I've ever tasted. It's a hard, spiny member of the melon family; the scent of the football-size fruit alone will take down a grown man faster than Sugar Ray Leonard. Imagine a slightly sweet onion, rotting for weeks in the hot sun. Now multiply that smell by 100 and you've got durian.

~Rambutan. These small, red, pom-pom-like fruits are native to Asia. Their translucent flesh is white or pink and tastes sweet. Eater beware: Each fruit contains a soft, crunchy seed, which is mildly poisonous when raw. If it's cooked, you'll be fine.

~Miracle fruit. This edible, *Synsepalum dulcificum,* earned its nickname due to an unusual characteristic: it makes sour foods taste sweet. You can actually suck on a lemon after chewing on miracle fruit and override the lemon's puckering qualities.

~Ugly fruit. This big, rugged, and gnarled fruit native to Jamaica deserves its name. However, it has a wonderful sweet and citrusy flavor. Let's just say the ugly fruit might not be much to look at, but it has a great personality.

~Cherimoya. Resembling a misshapen artichoke, the cherimoya has a sweet-sour taste comparable to a pineapple-banana-strawberry mix. Sounds delicious, but now consider that its crushed seeds are poisonous and its bark can induce paralysis when injected. Still hungry? Didn't think so.

~Square watermelon. The first square watermelons were thought to have been produced by a Japanese farmer and have been sold for upwards of eighty dollars a pop. However, it turns out the melons were grown in square molds on the vine—forcing them into perfect square shapes. So I guess these fruits aren't actually that weird. (They're just a big rip-off.)

the car. And don't ever drive away in a hurry—especially when you have yet to sample your purchase. If it's disappointing to your palate, you haven't lost anything. No matter where you taste the purchase, at the curb or an hour's drive away, you're going to dispose of it if you don't like it, or stop eating it, or give it to someone else who is going to enjoy it, probably in reverse order. But if it's new to you and you love it, you're going to want to eat a lot of it. I always sample at the curb.

One bite of achachairu sent me into a frenzy. They came in little one-kilo bags with roughly twenty fruits inside. I bought three bags and finished them within hours. That night, I ventured to the village market, bought three more bags, and brought them back to the room. I pounded those down in a day.

On the way back to the airport, I bought five more bags. By this time, I had convinced the crew that maybe they would want to eat some, and over the course of the next couple hours we demolished three of the bags. Just before we headed to the airport, I made a pit stop for a few more bags. My passion for fruit knows no bounds. I ate two more bags in the airport. If I could have taken them back to La Paz, I would have. Sadly, I couldn't buy enough, couldn't hold enough, and couldn't bring enough onto the airplane. I was eating every single piece of achachairu that I could.

Cultural elitism, price, and difficulty in procuring a certain ingredient can give food an artificially heightened sense of scarcity. However, where there is sunshine and water, there is fruit. Fruit is a very egalitarian edible, and obtaining it doesn't require special privilege—just a keen eye in a field if you're foraging, or a few cents if you're shopping in a market. Unless you're after a two-hundred-dollar square watermelon in Tokyo, fruit offers the best bang for the buck when it comes to exciting ingredients. Fruit also teaches us all a lesson in immediacy politics—there's a "carpe diem" quality that other foods don't have. Eat it when it's ripe, or miss your moment forever. And never pass up the fruit stand unless you know something that I don't.

Pleasant Surprises: A Gallimaufry

Since childhood, I'd dreamed of seeing the **Great Barrier Reef,** off the coast of Queensland, Australia. When I had the opportunity to travel there as an adult, I regressed to that giddy little kid staring out the window of my New York City apartment, dreaming of the world. Surfing, sharks, amazing snorkeling—what's not to love? Few more incredible natural structures exist than this coral reef that edges almost the entire northeastern coast of the Australian landmass.

> The Great Barrier Reef is one of the seven wonders of the natural world. It's larger than the Great Wall of China and the only living thing on earth visible from outer space.

I was stunned to discover just how far offshore the reef is located. Operators run giant diving barges with semipermanent structures floating above the reef; these support the massive influx of annual visitors, who are ferried in and out. There is no question about it: Pressure on a reef kills it. Activity in the water equals damage. The growth of the shipping lanes and commercial fishing, combined with the environmental circumstances of global warming, have resulted in a less productive and less vibrant reef. That being said, the Great Barrier Reef is one of the top ten **attractions** in the world, as

 The main industry on the Great Barrier Reef is tourism, which reportedly generates $1 billion annually.

far as I'm concerned. My palms were sweating as the crew and I boarded our boat in Cairns for the two-hour trip to our dive spot.

INTO THE REEF I GO. . . .

My diving companion was a gentleman named Lurch. He was a crazy Australian if ever there was one, a carefree guy who'd spent his formative years on the water, where his family made their living. Now he's stuck with the family business, resulting in days filled with free diving for fish, equipped with only a mask, an incredible oversize spear gun, and a pair of flippers. We finally arrived at our diving spot, where Lurch instructed me to start putting on my gear. As I dealt with my equipment, Lurch gave me a fifteen-minute tour of the shark bites and moray eel stings that covered his body. (I think this was an intimidation technique, and, frankly, it kind of worked.) However, this was a once-in-a-lifetime experience and I didn't have time to freak out, so over the side we went.

Lurch and I have the same idea of a good time. We spent a couple of hours in the water, pulling up as many crustaceans and mollusks as we could. We got a giant coral trout for the grill and a beautiful Spanish mackerel, but the real star of our lunch was a rainbow crayfish—or a *proper* rainbow crayfish, as Lurch likes to say.

Often referred to as painted lobsters, these creatures are actually members of the crayfish family. When I hear the name "crayfish," I think of some mudbug down in Louisiana, boiled with a mess of corn, potatoes, sausage, garlic, and onions. This is one of my favorite food treats, and I was expecting to experience the Down Under versions with the hundreds of crayfish we were to collect that day. Lurch kept looking under these giant rock overhangs in about eighteen to twenty feet of water, where most of the hefty ones live. He pulled out the first couple, showed them to me underwater, and signaled that they were too small to keep. I was stunned. These crayfish were the length of my arm, with a tail as big as my forearm. These were no mudbugs; they looked like giant tropical lobsters, complete with brilliant blue, red, and orange flanging all along their exoskeletal armor.

Lurch finally found one big rainbow crayfish, weighing in at about two and a half pounds. This massive beast was lunch. I'm a New England lobster guy and I just assumed this lobster was going to be roasted whole. Lurch had another idea. He brought a small pan to put on top of the grill. Next, he dabbed a tablespoon of butter in it, twisted off the lobster tail, cut the tip of the tail off the rear fin flaps, pushed this giant two-pound raw lobster steak out of the tube of skeleton that it lives in, chopped it into one-inch chunks, and pan-fried the meat in browned butter, finishing it off with a generous squirt of lemon.

We sat there on the beach while the Spanish mackerel, the kingfish, and the coral trout cooked. I tolerate warm-water lobster. The North Atlantic *Homarus americanus* is my kind of crustacean. However, the second-best lobster I've ever had is that rainbow crayfish from the Great Barrier Reef.

Rainbow crays are one of those delicious foods that you can find only down in Australia and some of the island countries just north of it. They have them in Indonesia and in

Okinawa, Japan, but physically plucking them from the **Great Barrier Reef** with a man who has spent his life diving there is an experience I wish for everyone.

A complex ecosystem, the Great Barrier Reef is home to the world's largest population of corals, coral sponges, mollusks, rays, and dolphins. There are over fifteen hundred species of tropical fish, more than two hundred types of birds, and about twenty types of reptiles, including sea turtles.

While people Down Under speak English, nonnatives might want to check out this crash course in Aussie slang.

Barbie: A barbecue. Very popular in Australia. Example: "Throw another shrimp on the barbie, Lurch!"

Blue: Fight. Example: "He was having a blue with his brother."

Bottler: An expression for someone who performs well. Example: "When it comes to eating weird food, he's a little bottler."

Sanger: Sandwich. Also sango. Example: "I'd like some Vegemite on my sango."

Chips: French fries. Example: "Would you like some chips with your sango?"

Earbashing: Nagging, nonstop chatter. Example: "My mom kept earbashing me to clean my room."

Grundies: Underpants. Example: "Hope you brought a clean pair of grundies."

Lolly: Candy. Lolly water is soda. A trough lolly is a perfumed urinal cake.

Oldies: Parents. Example: "I'd love to go, but have to ask my oldies first."

Pozzy: A position or spot. Example: "Let's find a good pozzy at the movie theater."

Spit chips: To be very angry. Example: "If you call me a moron one more time, I'm going to spit chips."

Stirrer: Not a wooden spoon but a troublemaker. To stir is to provoke someone. Example: "He is a stirrer."

"Who opened their lunch?": "Okay, who farted?"

CHILE

Speaking of seafood destinations, my favorite might surprise you. It isn't Australia, though I had a great time there. Japan certainly comes to mind, as do lots of places in Southeast Asia, or even the East Coast of the United States. But when it comes to seafood, Chile is a force to be reckoned with.

Chile is probably my favorite destination to recommend to any traveler, whether a well-seasoned one or someone heading abroad for the first time. Geographically diverse, financially sound, socially conscious, and certainly a very developed nation, Chile offers something for everyone. Gorgeous, relaxing beaches? After Brazil, Chile features the continent's longest coastline. Bustling cities? Santiago, a modern, pulsing Latin city, is a great global hot spot for everything from late-night dining and clubbing to historical tourism. If hiking and breathing the fresh mountain air are more your style, head to the Andes. The best part? All of this can be done on a shoestring.

And then there is the **seafood.**

 Chilean cuisine is a melting pot of techniques and flavors, influenced by Spain, Germany, Italy, Croatia, France, and the Middle East. Seafood is popular in Chilean dishes, since the country's western border is all coastline.

MERCADO CENTRAL

The cold Humboldt Current runs from the Antarctic Ocean along the Chilean coastline, creating a perfect environment for an abundant fishing industry. The quality and variety of the fish boggle the mind. One trip to **Mercado Central's seafood hall** in Santiago will confirm that Chileans are on top of their seafood game—gooseneck barnacles, abalone, pink-lipped angel clams, and loads of fresh fish. Exploring the Mercado Central is a singular experience. This is not one giant market, but several small specialty markets located within the hustle and bustle of the capital city. Whether you're looking for fresh produce, fine cuts of beef, or the country's best horse meat (yes, horse meat), you'll be sure to find it here.

The Mercado Central in Santiago was built between 1864 and 1872 as a place for artists to show their work. It quickly turned into a market center, though, and if you go there today, you'll find a variety of fresh food, especially sea products.

The market's seafood hall is a hub through which the greater part of Chile's seafood passes. Giant squid, conger eel, oysters the size of my hand, piles of mussels—you name it, if it swims, you'll find it at Mercado Central. People always ask me about the strangest food I've ever encountered. I think piure takes the cake. Piure is a giant sea squirt about the size of a small piece of luggage, and until this market trip, I'd never even heard of such a thing. If you were to encounter one in the ocean, you'd certainly cruise by it a million times, convinced it's a rock, not food. The best way to eat piure is raw, and the fishmonger slinging the stuff let me try it right there at the market. He took a huge serrated knife—really a sword, it was that huge—and sliced the animal into two giant halves.

Hundreds of pulsing, red, oyster-esque entities live within small nooks and crannies inside the coarse, spongy, rocklike carapace. You simply scoop them out with your fingers, squirt lemon or lime juice on them to both season and coincidentally stun the creatures (which, by the way, are alive and suctioned to your fingers), and pop them into your mouth. These little guys taste like a fish's rear end dipped in iodine. Not surprisingly, after a few bites, I loved it.

As strange as piure is, the item that sticks out most in my mind for sheer selfish eating pleasure is **picoroco.** This tube-like barnacle looks more like a minivolcano than like food. Throw these puppies on the grill and they essentially cook in their own shell. Ideally, you can place the shells directly on the coals underneath the grate.

 Picoroco, a giant barnacle, can be found living on the rocky shores of Chile and has the shape of a miniature volcano.

Once the barnacle is cooked, poke inside it and you'll find a white piece of meat that looks like a crab claw but tastes like lobster. You can eat this straight out of the shell, but often picoroco is found in soups. A bowl of cold tomato gazpacho filled with pieces of steamed picoroco is one of the most refreshing dishes you'll find on a hot day. Words to the wise: Don't hover over the grill too much if you are roasting them fresh. These little treats often become so hot that they explode, with seawater, pieces of barnacle, and hot shell spewing all over the place. Dodging a geyser of boiling-hot barnacle liquid isn't exactly the most comforting thing in the world, but it adds a sense of danger to the eating experience, which I like.

THE BEST PLACES TO EAT

With access to such fresh and abundant ingredients, it's not surprising Santiago offers incredible dining. The influx of Mapuche Indian and European influences shapes Santiago's highly regarded restaurant scene. From fine dining to street food, this city's got it covered, and I can't recommend a destination as one of my all-time faves without talking about some of my best-loved restaurants.

Picada Ana María is a humble little restaurant off Santiago's beaten path. A *picada* is Chile-speak for a casual restaurant—nothing overly fancy—serving simple, home-cooked meals. However, Picada Ana María gained so much popularity that they kicked the business up a notch, creating a full-service restaurant—complete with white tablecloths.

Ana María won't disclose how long she's been cooking,

but she's probably in her fifties, looks forty, and refuses to put her kitchen in the hands of anyone else. We ate eight or nine dishes there that were just spectacular. One in particular was the roasted partridge in a rosemary and honey sauce. While Ana María serves some fantastic salads and meat dishes, she's earned a reputation for serving incredible seafood, specializing in abalone.

Abalone are giant sea snails that live in thick shells adhered to rocks, usually in cold waters. Harvesting this meal is not an agreeable task. You have to sink into icy water equipped with a heavy iron bar to pry the abalone from the rock. Interestingly, this mollusk doesn't naturally grow in Chile, yet through aquaculture it is rapidly developing as a top industry. Chile is currently the fifth-largest producer of cultured abalone in the world, with 304 tons harvested in 2006.

 Abalone are sea snails that look like mussels or oysters. They're also called "ear-shells" for their oval shells, and can be used as decorations. Personally, I prefer to eat them.

When it comes to food preparation, abalone is known for its stubbornness and tough texture. Much like octopus, it's a type of dish best eaten raw, or you have to cook the heck out of it. Anything in between is inedible. Some chefs will tenderize it first, beating the meat over and over to break the muscle down. You can easily get carried away using a mallet and cutting board to tenderize the abalone, but you risk losing product or damaging the flesh.

Ana María has developed a unique method I had never encountered before. First, after placing five or six small fist-size pieces of abalone into a rubber tube, one of her prep cooks takes the ends as you'd hold a jump rope and smashes the tube on a cement sidewalk behind the kitchen. It's genius: The abalone doesn't go anywhere, because the centrifugal force keeps it in place. The amount of power delivered through the reverberation tenderizes the muscle in just a few smashes.

Next, the abalone are cleaned, trimmed, washed, and steamed. I tasted them cold and poached with a homemade lemon mayonnaise. These were easily the most tender abalone I've ever tried—definitely worth the flight to Santiago all by themselves.

I also sampled two versions of Ana María's pink razor clams. Until this trip, I'd seen these clams only in Japanese restaurants. Housed in an ovaloid, triangular shell with rounded edges, the clam is a beautiful pale pink color; one corner of the muscle is almost a fiery red, and the hue recedes into a gentle pink as the flesh goes deeper inside the apex of the shell. I ate them raw on the half shell with lemon, olive oil, and a bit of minced vegetable, as well as pan-roasted with white wine, garlic, and parsley. A simple, light, and delicious combination.

VALPARAÍSO

It's almost impossible to find a bad meal in Chile—with ingredients that fresh, meals need little fooling around with. The country's ultimate seafood spot might be Valparaíso. The actual city is a huge and industrial affair, outfitted with one of the largest port systems in the Southern Hemisphere.

However, a short drive outside the city brings you to fishing villages like Quintay, where you can watch boats coming into sleepy little coves carrying their seafood to local restaurants. Luckily, in Valparaíso there are many young chefs who pride themselves on their commitment to local food. The best conger eel I ate the whole week we were there came from a little restaurant called Café Urriola. Six seats, one chef, huge props. I've said it before, and I will certainly say it again: If seafood is your thing, Chile has got to be your country.

MY OTHER LOVE: PORK

I am nearly as wild about pork as I am about seafood. To me, pork preparation is an art form. However, with something so widely consumed around the world, it's hard to say that one bite of pig is any better than another.

I've experienced some really special porky goodness on a global scale, and it seems there is no shortage of ways to prepare this delicious creature. In Cuba, I enjoyed a pig finished with palmiche, the little fruits of the royal palm tree. I've dined on suckling pigs roasted to perfection in a three-hundred-year-old Madrid restaurant. I gorged myself on wild boar hunted down by Samoan tribesmen and buried with hot rocks covered with scraps of lamb fat for basting. The memory of whole roasted kahlua pig, cooked at a traditional Hawaiian luau underneath giant hot lava rocks with pulpy pounded roots of coconut palms, could never be wiped from my mind. These huge globs of vegetal matter dripped their sugary sap onto the heated rocks, which in turn gave the meat a sweet caramel flavor that, in my book, has never been replicated.

Pork barbecue occupies a whole different realm in the annals of swine artistry. So many cities are renowned for their special style of barbecue. The Memphis in May World Championship Barbecue Cooking Contest is the United States' pinnacle 'cue event, a time when the whole city becomes ground zero for the world's greatest barbecue talent. Kansas City, Missouri, may be considered the barbecue capital of the world, with biggies like Danny Edward's Eat It and Beat It, Earl Quick's, Gates Bar-B-Q, Arthur Bryant's, and Jack Stack, to name a few of my faves, all fighting for top honors in a city built on pork and beef BBQ.

PUERTO-RICO KNOWS ITS PORK

However, not one of those incredible experiences will ever measure up to my personal favorite. It didn't come from Hawaii, Samoa, Vietnam, Spain, or any of the other swine-centric hot spots around the globe. Surprisingly enough, it's the Puerto Ricans who make all other pork-worshiping cultures seem tame by comparison.

The Puerto Rican hillside village of Guavate serves as an **epicenter of pork** meals. Located an hour-and-a-half drive

> Guavate is inundated with *lechónerías* (roadside cafeterias whose specialty is seasoned, whole-roasted pig). Traditionally, the pig was roasted over an open flame mounted on a wooden spit called a *varita,* but these days, a steel spit is used.

outside of San Juan on Route 184 (known colloquially as the Pork Highway), Guavate is a great illustration for my theory that venturing out to the last stop on the subway is the best way to find the best foods, leaving the tourist traps in the dust and opening your mind to a more honest and authentic experience. Most of the time, the reward is a better meal, some smug satisfaction, and a better story when you get back home—at a minimum.

In Guavate I expected a little neighborhood with a couple of restaurants. Instead, I discovered a Puerto Rican village that lives and breathes *lechón asado,* roasted whole pig. On a Sunday afternoon, you share the pilgrimage to this pork mecca with hundreds of Puerto Ricans and clued-in tourists alike, who dine on the area's specialty and dance away the afternoon and evening to live salsa music.

A SPIRITUAL EXPERIENCE

Guavate restaurateurs are evangelical when it comes to the pig. In no place was this more evident than at El Rancho Original. This *lechónería* has spent generations perfecting the *lechón asado* process. The chefs finish the pigs on an orange, nut, and fruit diet. Once the animals are slaughtered, they are placed on giant wood-fired and wood-assist rotisseries, then turned for hours until every single part of the animal is perfectly cooked. Back in the day, the restaurant's reputation caused quite a stir throughout Puerto Rico and other Guavate restaurateurs cashed in, opening their own eateries along the same dusty little main street.

Today, about a dozen *lechónerías* line the street, serving

food cafeteria-style. Grab a tray and select a cut: pork belly, pork ribs, pork shoulder, pork chops, cheeks, ears, tails, hocks, and cracklings. The quality of the meat is fantastic—sweet, succulent, sticky, and fatty. The availability of so many different parts of the pig was the most exciting aspect of the meal. Any pig part is fair game, and you can pick a little bit of everything if sample platters are to your liking. The chefs simply place pig quarters on wooden chopping blocks. All you have to do is point to the piece you want. If they're running low, no sweat, they'll just grab another pig from the back. They are cooking them nonstop in a hell-bent pig-heaven tribute to your waistline expansion.

As fast as people can line up and fill their trays, the BBQers keep cooking up and slicing pig. In fact, at Christmastime, some of the restaurants have been known to go through nearly seventy pigs in a single day, each weighing in at roughly a hundred pounds. Of course, no Latin meal would be complete without fresh and plentiful sides. Beans, rice, cooked greens, yucca with garlic mojo, fried plantains—you name it, you get it alongside your pork.

Pick a spot under an open, breezy shelter created to protect diners from rain or the blazing sun, and plant yourself with your tray. Grab a napkin and dig in.

On Saturdays and Sundays, salsa bands perform while people eat, dance, and chat the day away. As rich and filling as the *lechón asado* is, the dancing certainly helps burn it off. Take a few bites of pork shoulder, get up and dance three or four numbers, sit back down, splash a little more chili sauce onto your barbecued pig, take a few more bites, and repeat. Oddly, while there are dozens of *lechónerías* to choose from, everyone is at El Rancho Original. You'd think the competition would be fierce, but it's a one-horse town as far as I am concerned.

Heladería de Lares

While the Puerto Ricans do a phenomenal *lechón,* I also have to give it to this small island when it comes to ice cream. Nothing beats *helado* (Spanish for ice cream) on a hot Caribbean day, and few people in the world do it better than Heladería de Lares. I've heard they have anywhere from five hundred to over a thousand flavors in their repertoire, but in any case, this shop is stocked with some amazing flavors. You could go with plain ol' vanilla or mint chocolate chip, but these guys are known for some seriously wacky creations. Here are my favorites—in no particular order:

Arroz con habichuelas: Rice and beans

Bacalao: Codfish

Zanahoria: Carrot

Batata: Sweet potato

Maíz: Corn

Ron: Rum

Coquito acanelado: Coconut flavored with cinnamon

Pollo: Chicken

Cerveza: Beer

Aguacate: Avocado

Camarón: Shrimp

Ajo: Garlic

Jengibre: Ginger

Heladería de Lares is located about an hour west of San Juan. Take Route 129 into Lares, then turn into the center of town. It's in the town's central square.

Unless you're eating a whole little baby suckling pig by yourself, you'll never have the opportunity to sample so many flavors on one plate. The rich and fatty belly is so much more toothsome than the leaner, luxury cuts like the chops. Compare that to the earthiness of the legs or to the way-too-rich-for-your-own-good cheeks. There's no doubt in my mind—if I had to eat pork in only one place, it would be in the little hillside town of Guavate, Puerto Rico.

DON'T FORGET ABOUT DRINKS!!

Beverages often provide a pleasant surprise—or an unpleasant one. In Bolivia, I sampled peanut juice for the first time, and it's something that I don't recommend to anybody. In Otavalo, Ecuador, I sipped aloe tonic, and I went through a struggle of grand proportions to keep that down. It's a nasty, bitter liquid filled with gel scraped from giant leaves of the aloe plant. At one point, I had a sticky, gooey strand extending from the pit of my stomach to the glass that held the elixir. That was when I almost lost it. I politely explained to the lovely aloe vendor that her drink must be an acquired taste, then quickly palmed it off on an elderly woman, who chugged the entire glass down in a matter of seconds.

I love **kvass,** a drink they practically give away on the streets of St. Petersburg. Called "baby beer" by the locals, this near-nonalcoholic beer is made with rye bread, and everyone from kids to the eighty-year-old babushkas drinks it. The Russians have a very strange relationship with alcohol.

 Kvass must be stored in a bottle, in a horizontal position, in the coldest possible place—ideally over ice. It is one of the national drinks of Russia.

I've had more types of chicha poured into a cup and thrown my way than I could ever begin to count. It seems every Latin American, South American, and Caribbean country has its own version, as do many African countries. Chicha is essentially a puree of water and some type of root vegetable, usually cassava or yucca, or maize. The drink is mildly alcoholic—maybe one one-thousandth of a percent—because it sits and ferments, and it is extremely fortifying, supplying a lot of healthful benefits from a probiotic standpoint.

From a psychological standpoint, I find a lot of these drinks challenging. I've seen families chew up two or three pounds of root vegetables, spitting the wet, masticated by-product into a giant pot of water, where it begins to slowly ferment. Families graciously offer you a glass of their home-made brew. At the end of a long, hot day, downing a glass of this stuff sounds like the last thing I'd want to do. However, no one ever said sharing food and experiencing culture is automatically easy, and with each brain-cramp-inducing gulp, I just chalk it up to a hard day at the office.

Despite some less-than-ideal beverage experiences, every

once in a while I come across a drink that just flips my trigger. Usually, it's the simplest stuff. The coffee in Nicaragua or Ethiopia's and Taiwan's teas are arguably the best in the world. I lost my mind over Ethiopia's mango smoothies—no ice cream, yogurt, or ice, just a puree of massive, juicy, fiber-free mangoes. Served chilled in a glass with a straw, this is a tremendous drinking pleasure. And I can't forget drinking fresh coconut water straight from the shell in the Philippines; it quenched my thirst like no other beverage. Skyr shakes in Iceland, avocado shakes in Chile—every country has some killer quaffables.

A TWIST ON SODA POP

However, when it comes to satisfying drinks, I'm a self-proclaimed soda pop junkie. Despite all these natural, one-of-a-kind experiences, I recall a bottled commercial soda pop beverage as being my all-time favorite.

On the road, especially in hot climates, I down water like it's going out of style. There's always that *Stay hydrated, stay hydrated* mantra replaying in my brain. At the end of my first day in Tanzania, I was just thirstier than I've ever been and way over drinking more water. In the afternoon we settled in at a small café in Arusha, and a waiter asked me if I wanted a Stoney. I'd never heard of such a thing. He looked at me and asked, "You've never heard of Stoney Tangawizi?"

With that, I demanded a Stoney immediately, if for no other reason than it had the most fun name I've ever heard. This oversize brown bottle, which looked like the old-school 7UP bottles, soon sat on the table in front of me.

The curvy bottle stood fourteen inches high, the thick glass sanded down around the outer edges, worn from being racked and cleaned so many times and refilled. And there on the side, in beautiful enameled letters, it said **"Stoney Tangawizi."**

> ¶¶¶ *Tangawizi* is the Swahili word for ginger. This popular ginger beer is a product of Coca-Cola. There is a Stoney Tangawizi Facebook fan page.

Most folks opt to sip from the bottle, often with a straw. I like to pour the drink into a glass over ice, or chug it straight. It's a perfect blend of ginger beer, ginger ale, and a very unfruity 7UP, with a nutty, sweet aftertaste. It has almost a sarsaparilla or root beer quality in the finish. If you're really thirsty and you're powering down a whole Stoney, the flavors play in your mouth like a quartet. Stoney is definitely my favorite drink in the world.

While I did find some Stoney in cans in South Africa, the version that hails from the Coca-Cola bottling plant in Tanzania does it the best. And just my luck, you can't find it anywhere else in the world.

I love pleasant surprises. Often they are the familiar food memories that come to me when I'm out of country rather than the shocking surprises or the anticipated foods. As much as I love Peking duck at Quanjude in Beijing, I expected it to be good, so it wasn't much of a surprise.

When I was seventeen years old, my friend Toby and I spent much of the summer on the Cycladic island of Sífnos, in Greece. We lived with a family on the island, and almost every day we ate at the local pizza parlor. Keep in mind that the Greek and Italian varieties of pizza hail from completely different families. The pizza we found in Sífnos started with a cooked piece of round dough, brushed with crushed tomatoes, salty Greek goat's cheese, and oregano, and drizzled with olive oil as it left the oven. It's more like a seasoned focaccia than anything else.

As a born-and-bred New Yorker, I'd like to think I'm an authority on great pizza, and I've thought about that delicious Sífnos pizza at least once a month for the last thirty years. One day I will get back there. Nothing would be a more pleasant surprise than discovering that more than three decades later, that Sífnos pizza joint is still putting out their simple, unexpected culinary gems.

SOME FINAL THOUGHTS

What does it mean to be a traveler, not a tourist? A traveler is filled with curiosity about the world we live in. A traveler realizes there are endless numbers of people to meet, places to see, and things to experience. A traveler steps outside his or her comfort zone, into unknown territory, with an open mind (and hopefully an empty stomach). At the end of the day, it is this curiosity about the world we live in that drives my actions, and ultimately fulfills me.

Through these experiences, I've gained a new perspective on what an ideal life is all about. As a kid in New York, I remember watching public television documentaries about tribal Africa. I'd think about how hard the people's lives were, how much better off I was, how sophisticated our big-city culture seemed to be. I felt superior and smug. Looking back, I can't believe what a little brat I was. I love my life, but is it the best, most fulfilling way to live? I'm not so sure.

Simplicity is something we Westerners tend to overlook when it comes to our day-to-day lives. However, the more people I meet and places I see, the more I've come to appreciate the little things. A simple shared meal with friends and family is truly one of life's greatest pleasures, and I've been humbled countless times by the generosity of those I meet on the road.

When I was filming in the Amazon jungle, my native guide Donaldo invited me to share a lunch at home with his family. He was so proud of his two-room home on stilts on the banks of the Napo River. We sat on the cooking room's floor, eating fried coconut grubs served on leaves, along with small steamed potatoes from his garden. He ate one grub, giving me two on my leaf, and also giving two to each of his three kids. Nine grubs and a few root vegetables were all they were going to get to eat that day. How do you explain that kindness and generosity?

From my experiences, it seems the secret to happiness is simply the ability to love and respect other people.

AUTHOR'S NOTE

Almost anything that crawls, swims, trots, runs, slithers, or flies has at one point crossed my lips. I'm always delighted to chat about the world of flavors I have encountered; how something tastes is more important than what something is. Like I always say, if it looks good, eat it.

What it's like to eat lamb brains (Morocco)
I've tried lamb brains many times. However, the experience that will forever be branded into my own brain was the time I sampled lamb brains in Morocco. Imagine: vendors pointing maniacally into vats of bubbling innards to attract customers. . . . It was spooky. The brains were boiled and served with cumin and salt on the side. You might think they would be rubbery, but they're actually rather creamy and taste like impossibly mushy river rocks.

Lamb brains are a delicacy not only in Northern Africa, but in many other parts of the world. Italians might use brains as stuffing for ravioli; Lebanese love to fry them with a little onion, salt, and pepper (it's a dish called nikha'at miqliyah, and it rocks!); and Indians often start their day with a breakfast of dosa (kind of like a crepe) stuffed with rice, lentils, veggies, and sometimes brains! The Chinese say eating brains will make you smarter, so eat some as your after-school snack and watch your grades soar.

What it's like to drink cow's blood (Tanzania)

In many cultures, drinking blood is considered an essential component of optimal health. The Masai tribe of Tanzania drink animal blood regularly. It's thought to make the body strong and keep you warm on a cool day. When you chug a glass of blood, your body temperature will rise a few degrees—seriously!

Freshly drained cow's blood tastes like sucking on a freshly used and discarded bandage the size of a dish towel. The blood is often collected at dawn and drunk for breakfast. A tourniquet is tied around the neck of the cow, allowing the blood to pool. Then, at close range, a tribesman shoots an arrow into the cow's jugular vein. Blood pours out of the wound into a gourd. After the cow has lost a few pints of blood, the wound is sealed shut by smearing it with the cow's own feces.

Drinking half a quart of this stuff was an act of desperation and hunger for me, but it's a typical Masai breakfast designed to deliver instant protein, like a power shake.

What it's like to eat donkey (China)

In the Western world, we tend to stick to the big three proteins: beef, pork, and chicken. The Chinese, however, are one of many Eastern cultures who give donkey meat two thumbs up. I've eaten it many times, and I can assure you that these folks are on to something.

Imagine the best steak you've ever feasted on; multiply that by ten, and you get donkey meat. It's truly one of my all-time favorite meats. It tastes a lot like veal—very delicate, with a hint of beefy flavor. The donkeys used aren't big like horses. They're a specific breed that's black-skinned and fairly small, like Shetland ponies. Try your donkey meat medium rare and I guarantee you'll go bananas for it.

What it's like to eat a giant fruit bat (Samoa)

What's your favorite after-school snack? Do you like to keep it healthy (an apple and peanut butter), or are you more of a junk food person (chips or cookies)? For kids in Samoa, roasted whole bat is a treat. I've seen kids fight over the last piece.

Roasted bat is an anomaly in the food world: The Samoans don't bother cleaning or gutting the bats prior to roasting them—because they don't have to. The innards of bats in that part of the world are extremely clean. However, the Samoans do make a crisscross incision in the animal's chest to allow steam to escape. The bats are then roasted over an open fire. The meat tastes like charred spoiled ham, gamy and metallic, fatty and almost sour in some places, and eating it is a fairly messy experience.

What it's like to eat dancing shrimp (Thailand)

Want to bring some serious fun to the dinner table? Try eating food that's alive. Nothing could be fresher—and freshness is the key to amazing seafood. My favorite example hands down is the Thai dish called dancing shrimp.

It starts out with small shrimp (about an inch long) that are still alive and kickin', along with a spicy, garlicky sauce; toasted rice powder; tomatoes; and fresh limes. When you squeeze the lime juice on the shrimp, the acidity makes them jump like crazy. This is when you start eating—if you can get ahold of one, that is!

This dish is so alive with flavor (no pun intended) that I wish I could eat it every day. Raw shrimp are like little briny gummy bears. And the toasted rice powder and chili-lime flavors are amazing.

What it's like to eat rotting shark meat (Iceland)

Hákarl, an Icelandic delicacy made of rotted shark meat, is one of the most horrific things I've ever experienced. This particular species of shark (Greenland or basking shark) is poisonous and is only edible after it has been buried in gravel, left to rot for at least two months, and then hung up to dry. Did I mention that this fish pees through its skin? It does, and it tastes like it. You can't imagine how nasty and ammoniacal this decaying creature is to eat. Icelanders might consider this a tasty treat, but I think I'll stick to hot dogs.

What it's like to eat durian (Asia)

Durian. The word makes me shudder. How can a simple fruit have such an offensive flavor? This fruit is slightly larger than a football and has a spiny husk that houses a flesh with the texture of rotten onions and the flavor of sweaty feet. The scent is so pungently rotten that durian is banned by law from many places, including shops, hotels, and public transportation. Why does anyone like this stuff? I just don't get it, but folks all over Asia are gaga about this fruity stink bomb.

What it's like to eat balut (Philippines)

Eating balut is psychologically petrifying. It's a hard-boiled egg with a fully formed duckling inside. You can see the duck's eyes, beak, and skeleton (there are even some fuzzy feathers chilling out in there!), and yes, you put the whole thing in your mouth and start chewing. When it's fresh, it tastes like a roasted piece of poultry in a hard-boiled egg seasoned with vinegar and salt. The flavor is fantastic. The trick is having the nerve to peel it and put it in your mouth without thinking too much.

What it's like to eat fattened duck liver (France, the United States)

Fattened duck or goose liver might sound like an odd thing to eat, but it's considered one of the world's most indulgent treats. This rich concoction usually goes by its French moniker, *foie gras* (pronounced "fwah grah").

Foie gras is one of my favorite foods. It's like butter made of meat; it's almost pure fat and has a smooth, velvety texture. If it was good enough for the pharaohs, it's good enough for me. I love liver, and this is the liver of the gods. One of the biggest culinary trends right now is the pairing of foie gras with everyday foods. Hot Doug's Sausage Emporium in Chicago offers a hot dog topped with it, and the Bazaar in Los Angeles does a foie gras lollipop—basically a bite of foie on a stick wrapped in a big puff of cotton candy. You shove the whole thing in your mouth at once. It's delicious.

What it's like to eat roasted baby sparrows (Vietnam, Taiwan)

If you're hungry on the go in the United States, you might buy a hot dog from a street vendor. In Vietnam and Taiwan, you'd buy whole roasted sparrows placed in a little to-go snack bag.

These crunchy little guys are roasted with skin, innards, and beak intact. They taste like great roasted chicken and crispy Chinese duck rolled into one. You pop the whole thing into your mouth—even the bones! They're delicate yet satisfying—heavenly. Who wouldn't love these?

What it's like to eat moose nose jelly (Alaska)

I love headcheese (meat jelly made from bits of flesh from a cow's or pig's head). Moose nose jelly is just a jellied loaf of headcheese made from—you guessed it—moose. On a trip to Alaska, I was asked to help make this gelatinous treat. "Sure," I said. "That sounds cool."

I thought we'd simply assemble already-picked bits from the moose's head. I was not prepared to see the whole head and neck of a 1,200-pound beast plopped down in front of me. We skinned the head and boiled it; then we picked out all the meat, fat, and connective tissue and boiled it in a giant vat. After that was done, the liquid from the vat was reduced and poured over the meat. It took hours, but it was sooooo worth it.

What it's like to eat a giant hissing cockroach (Thailand)

The idea of having a three-inch-long hissing cockroach on your tongue is psychologically daunting. But the fresh fried ones taste like giant Fritos, which helps get them down the hatch. Bugs are one of those things that look horrible but taste better than you think. I truly believe that anyone who tries fried cockroach or roasted grasshopper with a sprinkle of salt will wish they were packaged up and sold in their grocer's snack aisle. The bonus: They're an excellent source of protein!

What it's like to eat a tarantula (Cambodia)

These arachnids sound like a scary snack, but they taste like soft-shell crab—especially when they're fresh. The trick is digging them out of their underground lairs, defanging them without getting bitten, washing them, and then cooking them in a way that scorches off *all their hair*. It's really important to defuzz tarantulas before you eat them—the hairs carry a poison that can set your mouth on fire and numb your throat for days. When deep-fried first and then flash sautéed with sugar, salt, chilies, and garlic, the way they do in Skuon, Cambodia, they are addictively delicious.

What it's like to drink aloe juice (Ecuador)

Did you know that the plant used to cool a sunburn is available in drink form? The flavor is fine; the issue lies in the boogery three-foot-long threads of aloe scraped into the tonic. Having one end of the thread in your glass and one end in your stomach makes for a very barfable beverage.

What it's like to drink kopi luwak (Indonesia)

The thought of drinking coffee once bonded by poop may make your stomach percolate, but don't knock it till you try it. Kopi luwak is coffee derived from beans consumed, digested, and pooped out by the common palm civet, or luwak, a cat-sized mammal that sports the facial markings of a raccoon and is a relative of the mongoose.

This dung-derived delicacy is exported from the islands of Sumatra, Java, and Sulawesi in the Indonesian archipelago. Luwaks dine on ripe coffee cherries in Indonesia's treetops. The fruit is fully digested, while the bean remains intact and is excreted. Farmers then pluck the beans from the fecal matter. After a thorough scrubbing, they're roasted, ground, and brewed. The lewak's digestive process zaps the bitterness from the bean, creating a slightly sweet, rich flavor with less caffeine than your average cup of joe.

This is, bar none, the most superb, chocolaty, low-acid coffee I have ever tried. The fact that monkey-cats poop the beans out before natives collect them is a novelty that takes some getting used to . . . but the thing that's really hard to swallow is the price tag: a pound of beans costs over four hundred dollars!

What it's like to eat a beating frog's heart (Japan)

If you want to sample some of the oddest foods under one roof, check out a getemono bar in Japan. These eating establishments, frequented mostly by men, serve extremely unusual dishes; one of the strangest (and most popular) is frog sashimi.

The most difficult part of eating this dish is having to come face to face with your dinner prior to eating it. I selected my very own Kermit (still alive) before the skilled chef made fast work of skinning him. The chef also quickly plucked the still-beating heart from the frog's chest. Imagine trying to pick up a pulsating heart with your chopsticks—it wasn't easy.

I popped the whole heart into my mouth. It was a lot easier to get down than I'd expected. The frog's heart is small, tinny-tasting, and very soft when raw. It's almost flavorless, though, so it doesn't appeal to me much.

What it's like to eat dung beetles (Thailand)

Dung beetles themselves are light, crispy, and nutty—one of my favorite bugs to eat. Here's the catch: you have to fish dung beetles out of piles of fresh, steaming water buffalo poop. That's a big problem for most people. Ironically, people in northern Thailand, where this dish is a local favorite, dump them into a bucket of water when collecting them in the field not to rid them of the poop, but to keep their wings wet so they won't fly away!

What it's like to eat stinky tofu (Taiwan)

The Taiwanese are crazy about stinky tofu. The two-day-old soybean curd regularly sold on the street is delicious when split, grilled, stuffed with spicy cabbage, and basted in peanut sauce. I had it every day for lunch in Taiwan.

What's awful is the fourteen-day-old stuff at Dai's House of Unique Stink. These tofu squares sit for two weeks in a ten-year-old vegetal sludge that reminds me of Dumpster juice. The result is essentially inedible, so rancid and foul I could only try it once. I still have nightmares about it.

I hope this book inspires you to try something you think is gross—you just might like it!

ACKNOWLEDGMENTS

Charlie Conrad, Jenna Ciongoli, and the team at Random House who spearheaded the adult version of this book—their patience, tolerance, and understanding were limitless, and without their persistence and faith, there would be no book. A huge thanks goes out to Beverly Horowitz, Krista Vitola, and the team at Delacorte Press for not only seeing the potential to share my story with kids, but having the know-how to do so. You guys are amazing.